LACAN

ALSO AVAILABLE AT BLOOMSBURY

Critical Theory Between Klein and Lacan: A Dialogue
Amy Allen and Mari Ruti

Lacan Contra Foucault: Subjectivity, Sex, and Politics
Edited by Nadia Bou Ali and Rohit Goel

Lacanian Realism: Political and Clinical Psychoanalysis
Duane Rousselle

LACAN

A Genealogy

MIGUEL DE BEISTEGUI

BLOOMSBURY ACADEMIC
LONDON • NEW YORK • OXFORD • NEW DELHI • SYDNEY

BLOOMSBURY ACADEMIC
Bloomsbury Publishing Plc
50 Bedford Square, London, WC1B 3DP, UK
1385 Broadway, New York, NY 10018, USA
29 Earlsfort Terrace, Dublin 2, Ireland

BLOOMSBURY, BLOOMSBURY ACADEMIC and the Diana logo are trademarks of Bloomsbury Publishing Plc

First published in Great Britain 2021

Cover design by Ben Anslow
Cover image: Surviving Depression, 2008
Photograph by Anne Collier
© Anne Collier. Image courtesy of the artist; Anton Kern Gallery, New York; Galerie Neu, Berlin; Gladstone Gallery, Brussels; and The Modern Institute/ Toby Webster Ltd., Glasgow.

A catalogue record for this book is available from the British Library.

Library of Congress Cataloging-in-Publication Data

Names: Beistegui, Miguel de, 1966– author.
Title: Lacan : a genealogy / Miguel de Beistegui.
Description: London ; New York, NY : Bloomsbury Academic, 2021. |
Includes bibliographical references and index. |
Identifiers: LCCN 2020054503 (print) | LCCN 2020054504 (ebook) |
ISBN 9781350190771 (hardback) | ISBN 9781350190788 (ebook) |
ISBN 9781350190795 (epub)
Subjects: LCSH: Lacan, Jacques, 1901–1981. | Psychoanalysis.
Classification: LCC BF109.L28 B43 2021 (print) | LCC BF109.L28 (ebook) |
DDC 150.19/5—dc23
LC record available at https://lccn.loc.gov/2020054503
LC ebook record available at https://lccn.loc.gov/2020054504

ISBN: HB: 978-1-3501-9077-1
PB: 978-1-3501-9081-8
ePDF: 978-1-3501-9078-8
eBook: 978-1-3501-9079-5

Typeset by RefineCatch Limited, Bungay, Suffolk

To find out more about our authors and books visit www.bloomsbury.com and sign up for our newsletters.

For Slavoj Žižek

CONTENTS

LIST OF ABBREVIATIONS

Works by J. Lacan:

AE Jacques Lacan, *Autres écrits* (Paris: Éditions du Seuil, 2001).

E Jacques Lacan, *Écrits* (Paris: Éditions du Seuil, 1966). Trans. Bruce Fink, in collaboration with Héloïse Fink and Russell Grigg. *Écrits* (New York & London: W. W. Norton & Company, 2002).

PP *De la psychose paranoïaque dans ses rapports avec la personnalité* (Paris: Éditions du Seuil, 1975).

S I Jacques Lacan, *Le Séminaire livre I. Les écrits techniques de Freud (1953–1954)* (Paris: Éditions du Seuil, 1975). Trans. Tomaselli, S., with notes by Forrester, J. *The Seminar of Jacques Lacan, Book I: Freud's Papers on Techniques 1953–1954* (New York: Norton, 1991).

S II Jacques Lacan, *Le Séminaire livre II. Le moi dans la théorie de Freud et dans la technique de la psychanalyse (1954–1955)* (Paris: Éditions du Seuil, 1978). Trans. Tomaselli, S., with notes by Forrester, J. *The Seminar of Jacques Lacan, Book II: The Ego in Freud's Theory and in the Technique of Psychoanalysis 1954–1955* (New York and London: Norton, 1991).

S III Jacques Lacan, *Le Séminaire livre III. Les psychoses (1955–1956)* (Paris: Éditions du Seuil, 1981). Trans. and notes Grigg, R. *The Seminar of Jacques Lacan, Book III: The Psychoses 1955–1956* (London & New York: Routledge, 1993).

S IV Jacques Lacan, *Le Séminaire livre IV. La relation d'objet (1956–1957)* (Paris: Éditions du Seuil, 1998).

S VI Jacques Lacan, *Le Séminaire livre VI. Le désir et son interprétation (1958–1959)* (Paris: Éditions du Seuil, 2013).

S VII Jacques Lacan, *Le Séminaire livre VII. L'éthique de la psychanalyse (1959–1960)* (Paris: Éditions du Seuil, 1986). Trans. and notes Porter, D. *The Seminar of Jacques Lacan, Book VII: The Ethics of Psychonalysis*, 1959–1960 (London & New York: Routledge, 1999).

S VIII Jacques Lacan, *Le Séminaire livre VIII. Le transfert (1960–1961)* (Paris: Éditions du Seuil, 2001). Trans. Fink, B. *The Seminar of Jacques Lacan, Book VIII 1960–1961: Transference* (London: Polity, 2015).

S XI Jacques Lacan, *Le séminaire livre XI. Les quatre concepts fondamentaux de la psychoanalyse* (1964) (Paris: Éditions du Seuil, 1973). Trans. Sheridan, A. *The Seminar of Jacques Lacan, Book XI: The Four Fundamental Concepts of Psychoanalysis* (1964) (London & New York: Routledge, 2018).

S XVI Jacques Lacan, *Le Séminaire livre XVI. D'un Autre à l'autre (1968–1969)* (Paris: Éditions du Seuil, 2006).

S XVII Jacques Lacan, *Le Séminaire livre XVII. L'envers de la psychanalyse (1969–1970)* (Paris: Éditions du Seuil, 1991). Trans. and notes, Grigg, R. *The Seminar of Jacques Lacan, Book XVII: The Other Side of Psychoanalysis 1969–1970* (New York: Norton, 2007).

S XVIII Jacques Lacan, *Le Séminaire livre XVIII. D'un discours qui ne serait pas du semblant (1971)* (Paris: Éditions du Seuil, 2007).

S XIX Jacques Lacan, *Le Séminaire livre XIX. . . . ou pire* (1971–1972) (Paris: Éditions du Seuil, 2011). Edited by J.-A. Miller. *The Seminar of Jacques Lacan, Book XIX: . . . or Worse 1971–1972* (London: Polity, 2018).

S XX Jacques Lacan, *Le Séminaire livre XX. Encore (1972–1973)* (Paris: Éditions du Seuil, 1998). Trans. and notes Fink, B. *The Seminar of Jacques Lacan, Book XX: Encore – On Feminine Sexuality, the Limits of Love and Knowledge 1972*–1973 (New York: Norton, 1998).

S XXII Jacques Lacan, *Le Séminaire livre XXII. R.S.I. (1974–1975). Ornicar?*, 2–5, 1975. A full transcript of the seminars is also available here: http://www.valas.fr/IMG/pdf/s22_r.s.i.pdf.

S XXIII Jacques Lacan, *Le Séminaire livre XXIII. Le Sinthome (1975–1976)* (Paris: Éditions du Seuil, 2005). Trans. and notes Price, A. R. *The Seminar of Jacques Lacan, Book XXIII: The Sinthome 1975–1976* (London: Polity, 2016).

All abbreviations will be followed by the French and English pagination (when available).

Works by S. Freud:

SE *The Standard Edition of the Complete Psychological Works of Sigmund Freud* (London: Vintage, 2001).

Introduction

Lacan was fond of knots, of all kinds: loops, coils and braids; bow ties and cravats; tame and wild; Brunnian and Borromean. He enjoyed thinking about them, tying them around his neck and playing with them in his spare time. He was very much a nodophile and a nodologist, if not a nodomaniac. This was no coincidence: the knot, in its many forms and topological complexity, is the (often complex, if not obscure) image that best represents – a Kantian would say: schematizes – the reality with which he struggled all his life, namely, desire. And it took him a while to recognize it as such. The knot, he claims, is the very object of analytic discourse, and therefore the form in which it is best represented. But, I insist, it is only an approximation, and an image, not unlike those Bergson multiplies in his attempt to describe the qualitative reality of duration. Where the schema, and even the symbol, are meant to yoke together a concept or an Idea and an intuition in a clear and distinct image, the Lacanian knot provides a blurred and moving image of desire as signalling the 'opacity' of consciousness, of what lives and bubbles beneath its surface. When it does surface, it is in the form of a speech (a *parole*) we don't control and a body we don't command, actions we neither intended nor anticipated, symptoms that creep up on us, as if carried out by an alien self. It is the form of a truth we don't recognize and often want nothing to do with, an uncomfortable, at times painful truth we would rather sit on than confront. The knot of desire signals this interlacing of the self and the alien, the surface and the depth, truth and deception. In 1972, for example, Lacan saw the three registers of the Real, the Imaginary and the Symbolic as woven together into a knot or chain, and held together differently according to the prevalence of one of the registers over the other two, and this in such a way that by untying one the other two also come undone.[1] Subsequently, in *Le Sinthome* (1975–1976), he explored other types of knotting, and especially one involving four elements, with the symptom as the ring of string (*rond de ficelle*) that holds the other three together.[2] Needless to say, desire is not something we can easily represent or imagine, and the knot, if it is at all an image, is one that appears tighter and more complex as we approach it. It can't be explained or explicated, flattened as it were. But it can be explored, entangled and its threads exposed.

Lacan's thought was expressed first and foremost as a *parole vivante*, a living voice seeking itself out, surging forth and falling back, progressing and regressing, plunging into the depths of the unconscious and coming back to the surface sometimes with rare pearls, other times with mere grains of sand. Unsurprisingly, reading Lacan is a mixed experience: it is like being sucked into a vortex, having one's mind stretched and bent, forced into a state of – at times exhilarating, at times frustrating – confusion. All the names and schemas he introduced at various points to schematize the obscure, split subject of desire (the Other, the phallus, the Thing, the object small a, etc.) were just that, and never quite the thing itself, the real deal. The Real does not so much exist as 'insist', *at the limit* of the Imaginary and the Symbolic. It signals the 'presence' of a crack, a gaping hole at the heart of subjectivity, one that is visible only through the imaginary and symbolic effects it produces, or the events that escape from its force of attraction. It is the Impossible itself: unreachable, unimaginable, half-known and half-said. That is its consistency, that in which it consists.[3] As such, and unlike what we normally call reality (*la réalité*), it can't be intended, perceived or represented, made the object of what phenomenologists call an intuition, through which something is given in the flesh as it were, *leiblich*. The Real is what we come up against, at the limit of language and consciousness. It is not one of those 'things' (*Sachen*) to which, phenomenology claims, we can 'return'.

As for the question of desire itself, its justification is a function of its ability to unlock the gates of human subjectivity: desire is the mechanism through which we *become* subjects, that is, through which we experience, understand and comport ourselves as subjects. But this can immediately be understood in two, very different ways, which constitute the tension that runs throughout this book, indeed constitute it as a transcendental or quasi transcendental claim, for which desire signals the basic structure or essence of the unconscious; as a historical claim, for which desire constitutes something like a historical a priori or unconscious, a complex and contingent combination of discourses and institutions that shaped the western subject into a desiring subject. In both instances, desire operates as the condition of possibility of a range of representations, actions and institutions, and the reality simmering beneath the surface of this fiction we call the self. As such, the distance separating genesis and structure, or history and the transcendental, is not that great, and becomes a real issue only when we begin to ask about the possibility of extracting ourselves from the specific configurations or regimes of desire in which we find ourselves, in order to desire differently, or perhaps not desire at all.

One needs a way into this labyrinth, a *method* if not to untie this knot, at least to identify its threads and understand how they are woven together. Mine will be genealogical and critical.[4] Its point of departure is a specific historical period – I would tend to call it an event – that took place over a few decades between the end of the eighteenth and the middle of the nineteenth centuries. Lacan engaged with it throughout his life, sometimes explicitly, sometimes only implicitly. Having explored it systematically elsewhere, I will be brief here.[5] The event in question consists in the normalization or normativization of the western subject of desire, that is, the progressive insertion of the subject of desire within a precise and elaborate *system* of norms that required the emergence of new rationalities and specific regimes of power, designed to enforce the rational norms in question. Let me explain.

Beginning with early Christianity, and Augustine especially, and until the middle of the eighteenth century, the subject of desire – the emergence and evolution of which in western practices of the self and discourses of truth would need to be specified – was defined in relation to the order of interdiction and the power of the law, around which, so often and for so long, the problem of government and, more generally, that of power, were (and still are) articulated.[6] As Foucault puts it in the first volume of *The History of Sexuality*, and most certainly with (a certain) Lacan in mind, according to this 'juridico-discursive' model of desire, 'the law is what constitutes desire and the lack on which it is predicated'.[7] As a result, the only two tactics available, which genealogy is precisely to question and overcome, are the 'promise of a "liberation"' – if, as Marcuse argues, 'power is seen as having only an external hold on desire' – or 'the affirmation: you are always-already trapped' – if the law is 'constitutive of desire itself'.[8] Foucault sharpens his critique of this juridical model of power, especially when applied to the problem of desire, by emphasizing the false alternatives to which it leads:

> But the problem is not to know whether desire is alien to power, whether it is prior to the law, as is often thought to be the case, or whether it is the law that, on the contrary, constitutes it. This question is beside the point. Whether desire is this or that, in any case one continues to conceive of it in relation to a power that is always juridical and discursive, a power that has its central point in the enunciation of the law. One remains attached to a certain image of power-law, or power sovereignty, which was traced out by theoreticians of right and the monarchic institution.[9]

Foucault has a point: the western morphology of desire, the roots of which actually go deeper than the monarchic institution, is very much bound up with the paradigm of the Law, especially in its moral and religious sense. And as we'll see, Lacan engaged and struggled with this paradigm, whether in its Pauline or Kantian form, throughout much of his life, at times adopting it, at times problematizing it. Foucault concludes his critique by saying that it is this juridical-discursive image of power, this model of sovereignty, which we must break free of, 'if we wish to analyze power within the concrete and historical framework of its operation'.[10] I want to suggest that the analytics of power in question, which 'no longer takes law as a model and a code',[11] is one that, in fact, emerged over the past two centuries and defined the event I spoke of earlier, to the point of shaping and governing the subject of desire today, of constructing the subject of desire *as* a subject of governmentality. In other words, my claim is that the contemporary subject of desire is defined less by the power of the law – be it that of God, the sovereign or one's conscience – and more by that of the norm. Desire is seen less as a force to be controlled, dominated or punished, through a spiritual or moral therapy, as that over which one needs to exercise one's sovereignty and will, and more as a set of tendencies that can deviate from their natural norm, and thus be subjected to a system of correction and rectification, thus to something resembling an orthopaedics of the self. The difference between the two, of course, is that whereas one transgresses a law, one only deviates from a norm. Here the meaning of norm is the same as the Latin *norma*: a straight angle that allows one to 'straighten' something – something that, for various reasons, may have deviated from the normal, becomes abnormal. The norm – normative power – does not aim to exclude, reject or repress. On the contrary: its primary aim is to redress, correct, rectify, reintegrate, rehabilitate, in short, normalize. The type of power that is at issue here isn't repressive or conservative, but productive and inventive: in order to operate, it requires new types of knowledge and new institutions. In short, whereas a law forbids certain acts, without transforming their subject, the norm generates a form of subjectivity.

This normalization of desire coincided with the emergence of three discourses and disciplines, as well as the creation or transformation of various institutions, all of which, at one point or another, Lacan engaged with. To be sure, the analytic in question, at least in its modern version, took the form of a science of sexuality and included the (highly significant) clinical understanding of desire as defined by a 'normal' sexual instinct, which, through a series of deviations, was thought to lead to 'abnormal', pathological behaviours known as 'perversions'. This clinic of desire emerged in the context of the birth of psychiatry, psychopathology and medico-legal science in the nineteenth century, and coincided with a naturalization of desire and the invention of the *homo sexualis*. But the normative analytic of desire exceeds its sexual dimension. In the late eighteenth century, the subject of desire underwent a radical transformation of a different, yet related kind: through the construction of a new rationality – political economy – and a transformation of the place and role of the market, the modern subject began to understand and experience themselves as a subject of 'interest' and 'utility'. Desire was recognized as an irreducible and necessary engine of agency, but only in the form of economic self-interest. These newly formed norms, which were subsequently followed by those of efficiency, productivity, flexibility and human capital, helped create the modern bourgeois order and the *homo economicus*. Finally, through the originally philosophical, and subsequently psychological, legal and socio-political concepts of self-love, self-respect and self-esteem, the modern subject began to experience its own subjectivity as essentially motivated by a desire for recognition – recognition not of its qualities and achievements, but its intrinsic worth and value *qua* human being. Adam Smith describes this longing to be recognized as a subject, that is, to be acknowledged and count for something as 'the most ardent desire of human nature'.[12]

The transformation of the subject of desire translated into the emergence of not only the *homo economicus* and the *homo sexualis*, but also the *homo symbolicus*. More recently, neo-Hegelian liberals such as Francis Fukuyama, Charles Taylor and Axel Honneth have sought to turn the desire and demand for recognition into an essential pillar of liberalism, and indeed the social and political dimension that the purely economic form of liberalism failed to perceive and integrate. What those various regimes of desire have in common is their normativity: they are not only rationalities that produce concepts through which we gain a new understanding of who we are, and a new experience of ourselves; they are also structures of power, which operate through institutions such as the market, the family, hospitals, schools and universities, and through which bodies and minds are altered, shaped, governed, in short, normalized.

How are we to read Lacan's theory of desire in relation to that evolution? Does it simply find its place within that analytic, and negotiate some of its terms, or does it seek to question, displace or subvert it? Is his theory of the subject an extension and deepening of that system, a further way of chaining the subject to the power of the norm? Or is it an attempt to twist free of it, to offer a conception of desire that minimizes its effects of power, and its commitment to the morphology of truth that is at the heart of normative power? Is it, to use his own late terminology, an instance of the master's discourse, or its reversal and a systematic opposition to relations of domination, whether of psychiatric power, capitalism or even the politics of recognition? If, as Foucault claims, critique can be understood as the ability 'to question truth on its effects of power and question power on its discourses of truth',[13] should Lacan's discourse (the analytic discourse) not also be defined as critical? But how could such a resistance be carried out if, following Lacan, we *begin* with a theory of the subject, rather than with the relations of power and the procedures of truth through which subjects are constituted; with a constituent subject, understood as structure, from which the contingent, the eventful has been evacuated, only to be historicized subsequently, rather than with the differentiated and discontinuous history through which the subject is constituted? Furthermore, if analytic discourse is itself a discourse of truth, how can we define the system of truth that underpins it? Does its concept of truth simply extend that of the other discourses, or question it? And does genealogy itself seek to criticize that discourse in the name of another truth, another, 'better' regime of truth? Or does it situate itself outside truth, outside the play or game of truth, in order to see better the point at which truth connects with various instances of power, deepening and reinforcing them?

Those questions call for nuanced and provisional answers. To be sure, Lacan resists the 'sexualization' of desire. In fact, he (famously and repeatedly) went as far as to claim that 'there is no sexual relationship [*il n'y a pas de rapport sexuel*]', for the simple reason that the sexual act only fills the hole *(le trou)* that defines the (relational) subject.[14] The sooner we understand this, he says in substance, the sooner we're able to confront the reality of desire, that is, the unconscious as 'the Real'. At the same time, and by that I mean in his very effort to turn to the matter of desire, and to the reality of an essentially split or punctured (*troué*) subject, Lacan turns it into a problem of imaginary recognition, which is another pillar of liberal governmentality. Similarly, and from the very start, he resists the naturalization of desire, but at the cost of subjecting desire to the power of the Law, and thus to the (symbolic) paradigm of sovereignty. In the 1950s, he seems to justify a form of authoritarian power, symbolized in the figure of the Father, and reflected perhaps in that of the analyst himself. Yet his later work provides a critique of the illusion (or fantasy) of sovereignty, of power as omnipotence and autonomy, and of the type of knowing (*savoir*) rooted in such a fantasy: the *savoir* of the master. In fact, it gnaws away at the *Ich Ideal*, or the process of identification with the figures of authority and power, such as the Father, the Master or the Analyst. Ultimately, the analyst is not a knowing or knowledgeable subject, but a subject who is 'supposed to know'.[15] And the discourse of the analyst is not even a discourse of truth. Or at least, it is uncertain about its own relation to truth, which it problematizes: once severed from the Cartesian legacy, which understands truth as *certainty* and marks the beginning of modern science, 'what', Lacan asks in conclusion to Seminar XI, 'is the order of truth which our praxis engenders?'.[16] If the discourse of psychoanalysis signals something 'beyond science', 'how can we be sure that we aren't engaged in an imposture?'.[17] By situating the discourse of psychoanalysis outside what Lacan calls *La* science, does he condemn it to being a mere simulacrum of truth, and the analytic training and cure a 'ceremony' (256) or 'religion' (294) based on 'belief' (*croyance*) (294)?[18] Or does he situate it outside both Science and Religion, opening up a new space of discourse, in which the nature of subjectivity itself is at stake? Finally, Lacan resists what I would call the commodification of desire and the norms of utility, productivity, interest, efficiency and flexibility. which define the rationality of liberal political economy. And his own concept of *jouissance* is deployed against that of pleasure, especially in its utilitarian appropriation. But he also, and until the very end, insists that lack structures desire. In short, whilst speaking from within much of that analytic, he develops tools to engage with it both immanently and critically, that is, with a view to asking how we are made to desire *today*, the sort of subject we have become and the place of psychoanalysis as a counter-discourse.

Freud, of course, had paved the way for a critical assessment of the highly restrictive and normative construction of the sexual subject, as inherited from the psychopathology of the second half of the nineteenth century. Whilst retaining the overall epistemological framework of sexuality, his writings offer a way out of the psychiatric discourse of the natural instinct and of perversions as essentially pathological. In fact, he offers a double way out, one from the top as it were, and one from the bottom. On the one hand, through his analysis of child sexuality, and of its pre-genital, polymorphously perverse dimension, Freud recognizes 'normal', that is, adult, genital and reproductive sexuality as the result of a perhaps necessary but in any event costly process of normalization: through repression and sublimation, the libido is made compatible with the demands of 'civilization', without ever renouncing the principle of pleasure that governed infantile sexuality and psychical life. On the other hand, from 'Beyond the Pleasure Principle' (1920) onward, Freud is forced to recognize the existence of a drive that is itself not sexual, and thus not generated from within the economy of the pleasure principle. This is an essentially destructive form of desire, which can be oriented towards the self, or towards others, and takes the form of ambivalence, death wishes, sadism and masochism, but also war, organized cruelty and genocide. As such, it helps throw light on some of the disturbing behaviours we find in the literature, without situating them within the rationalities of either sexuality or liberal penology. It reveals the very limit of both, and forces the latter to explore its connection with what Lacan will eventually recognize as the connection of desire with the Law, and with what, following Foucault, I will call the juridical-discursive or sovereign paradigm of power.

Lacan's conception of desire, I want to argue, signals a further shift away from the analytic of sexuality, and a reorientation of desire towards (in chronological order) a *dialectic*, an *ethics*, and, finally, a *mathematics*. In other words, if Lacan is of particular interest to the genealogist of desire, it is because his conception and practice of psychoanalysis marks a point of bifurcation within the *scientia sexualis*, and opens up the space of a different articulation of desire. Unlike Reich or Marcuse, for example, he does not see the ills of our society as the result of a repression of sexuality, and does not therefore seek the liberation of sexuality as a way of overcoming such ills and bringing about a more harmonious society. On the contrary, he carries out the transition or mediation in question by shifting the clinical emphasis from the *normative* discourse of sexual instincts and perversions, which he judges to be rooted in a problematic naturalism and biologism, to an irreducible articulation (a 'knot' or 'entanglement') of desire and the law, or of desire through a legislative paradigm. In fact, and to be more precise, the articulation in question is twofold: to begin with, it refers to the symbolic order of prohibition, transgression and guilt; beyond or outside the dimension of the symbolic, however, it refers to the realm of the 'real' and 'the Thing', which is also that of ethics. If the law plays a crucial role in the latter configuration of desire, it's in a very different sense: not as what limits desire and provokes its drive to transgress, but as its purest expression. Kant was the first to formulate it in his practical philosophy: the true and ultimate expression of the faculty of desire, he claims, can be found not in our natural inclinations and the empirical or 'pathological' objects to which they correspond, but in its capacity to be determined by a causality that is entirely independent of any such inclination – a free causality. As such, the itinerary described below is that which takes Lacan from a (broadly speaking) Hegelian to a (broadly speaking) Kantian model. But does the moral law exhaust the designation of the real as what falls outside the symbolic, or as what cannot be symbolized? If not, can there be a discourse of the real, or does the real signal the limit of language itself, that of which we cannot speak, yet which we always speak, that which cannot be integrated fully into a discourse (*le discours*), yet takes the form of speech (*la parole*)?

This does not mean that the vocabulary of perversion, central to the analytic of the nineteenth and early twentieth century, disappears altogether from Lacan's text. Far from it: he describes homosexuality as a perversion, and one that the Greeks 'sublimated' by turning it into a 'cultural fact' (*fait de culture*) and a 'construction', if not an art.[19] Yet, Lacan no longer defines perversions on the basis of a narrow – that is, genital, heterosexual and procreative – understanding of 'normal' sexuality. He loosens the grip of the normative (and naturalism) on desire, but only to tie the latter – and for a time only – to its legislative (or symbolic and archaic) regime. The key question in the end, is no longer, or at least primarily, that of the normal and abnormal (or perverse) behaviour, and that of the therapeutic, normalizing techniques through which the patient can be made normal again (or for the first time). It is not the question of the conflict between normal and pathological instincts, or even between basic drives, such as *eros* and *thanatos*. Rather, it is the question of the conflict between the narcissistic (and violent) tendencies of an Ego that seeks to be everywhere at home in the world, and everywhere itself, and the Law of an Other that speaks from on-high and beyond, and limits its power absolutely. In that respect, Lacan can be seen as mediating between the clinic of the instincts, inherited from the nineteenth century, and the philosophical ethics of desire, inherited from the Enlightenment, and from Kant especially. Lacanian psychoanalysis – and by that I mean both the analytic and clinic of desire for which it stands – is a humanism, but a humanism 'of the other Man', to use Levinas's expression. The ethics of psychoanalysis refer to both a practice, that of analysis, which involves a singular relation of *parole* and address between the analyst and the *analysand*, and a theory of Desire, articulated around the Law.[20] Not only does the discourse and clinic of psychoanalysis confirm the shift from the paradigm of the 'medical gaze' to the 'analytic ear', already introduced by Freud; it also situates this practice in the context of ethics, and a shift away from an epistemology of norms and a naturalist science. This stage and development, which Lacan refers to as the 'tangled knot [*nœud étroit*] of Desire and the Law', reaches its peak in the early 1960s.[21]

But, as I will argue, it also signals a dead end, which Lacan will spend much time extricating himself from in his later work. The 'knot' of desire undergoes a third and final twist in the late 1960s and early 1970s, and, through a kind of topological turn, is recognized as the very image of desire itself. In what may appear like a paradox, that period can also be seen as a contribution to a more explicit historical critique of desire, and especially to the manner in which the analytic of desire intersects with the Marxist critique of political economy. To be more specific, with his concept of *plus-de-jouir*, or surplus enjoyment, and its deep connection with that of the object *a*, Lacan is able to show the relevance of the analytic of desire for a critique of the type of subjectivation that corresponds to late capitalism, and thus for a critique of political economy. In that respect, his work connects with that of Reich and Marcuse, without falling into the illusion of a post-capitalist 'liberation' of 'sexual' desire, or a liberation of sexual desire as a way of overcoming an essentially 'repressed' society. In that, his position is closer to that developed by Foucault in the first volume of *History of Sexuality* and can, to an extent, be seen as a contribution to a *genealogy* of desire: the articulation of desire and power is irreducible, and the idea of a 'free' or entirely emancipated desire is illusory. This, however, should not stop us from distinguishing and discriminating between actual, historical regimes of desire, on the basis of the power relations they involve, and the effects of subjectivation they generate. At the same time, whereas Foucault does not see the possibilities of resistance to the analytic of desire from within, and seeks alternative processes of subjectivation through a range of techniques or 'technologies' of the self, Lacan wants to retain desire as the central axis around which subjectivity revolves and transforms itself.

Bearing in mind Foucault's claim regarding the manner in which, beginning in the late eighteenth century, desire is naturalized, and integrated into the double 'scientific' framework of political economy and psychiatry, I'll start by emphasizing the manner in which Lacan is keen to sever the link between desire and naturalism, in order to reveal the deeper mechanisms of identification and recognition that structure the unconscious (Chapters 1 and 2). But if those mechanisms can account for a certain stage of the development of the unconscious, and the narcissistic (and even paranoid-psychotic) tendencies that we all inherit, they don't account for their resolution, or the possibility of overcoming their intrinsic aggressiveness. It is only by introducing the symbolic value of the Law, against the backdrop of the Oedipal conflict, that Lacan is able to point to a way out of the dangers of narcissistic identification. I will illustrate this decisive shift by focusing on one article in particular, in which Lacan discusses the role of psychoanalysis in specific cases of crime and punishment – the very type of paranoid, murderous cases that marked the limit of liberal rationality, and the transition to the psychiatric style of reasoning (Chapter 3). Crucially, the focus on the article in question will also be an opportunity to raise the question of the status of truth in psychoanalysis, and the manner in which it forces one to distinguish between a subject of truth and a subject of knowledge, an alethurgy and an epistemology. Chapter 4 turns to Lacan's interpretation of the moral law in Kant as a way of coming to terms with the tension raised in the previous chapter, related to the transgression of the Law as both a form of *jouissance* and a demand for punishment. I will end the chapter by turning to Foucault's brief but key remarks regarding 'the political honour of psychoanalysis' at the end of the first volume of *History and Sexuality*, and suggest that, whilst perhaps justified in the context of an evaluation of the position of psychoanalysis on state racism, and biopower in general, they fail to integrate his own critique of the legislative and symbolic model of power (and desire), which he sought to overcome. In other words, I will end with some critical comments regarding the ethics of psychoanalysis, or the construction of psychoanalysis as an ethics – in fact, a morality – of the Law. But the book does not end on that critical note. In fact, those critical questions serve as a way into Lacan's later thought, which constitute a remarkable turning. In those later seminars, Lacan moves away from the paradigm of the Law, both formally and substantially. Formally, he develops a topological model of the unconscious, organized around the knot (*rond*), or the round of knot (*rond de ficelle*). Substantially, he either reworks or introduces concepts such as the object *a* and *jouissance* (in the form *plus-de-jouir*), which allows his thought to become more historical and critical, and find an original proximity with that of Marx (Chapter 5). This later development, I will suggest, requires that we return to the status of the Real as the fundamental dimension of the subject of desire.

As a newcomer in the field of Lacanian studies, I have relied on many scholars to guide me through his writings and seminars. At times, I felt the need to disagree with them, and engage critically with others. Some readers will wonder about my lack of engagement with Badiou as a reader of Lacan. I therefore feel the need to say a few things in anticipation. From a philosophical perspective, Badiou is arguably the most original interpreter of Lacan's work of the past 40 years.[22] The speculative, and specifically ontological light he sheds on the Lacanian corpus, whilst also attempting to draw the consequences of the 'antiphilosophical' challenge that the Lacanian corpus poses for philosophy, and the conditions under which philosophy remains possible *after* Lacan, has revolutionized the reception of Lacan. Yet, the genealogical approach I privilege here is far removed from the formalistic approach he favours. For Badiou, the historical significance of Lacan lies in the 'heroic' manner in which, at a time in which the categories of the subject and truth are either entirely foreclosed, or subjected to a form of scepticism born of the inability to measure up to the Platonic destiny of philosophy, the French psychoanalyst insists on constructing a new and strong concept of the subject – not the subject which, from Descartes to Husserl, was conceived as 'the source or locus of truth', but the subject understood as 'a fragment of truth'.[23] This is very different from the genealogical approach, which is concerned with processes of subjectivation, or the production of subjective effects. Badiou is concerned with the articulation of truth and subjectivity beyond its Heideggerian, Althusserian or Lyotardian critique (the latter of which he considers emblematic of the *grande sophistique* of our time). For him, this means an articulation within a (necessarily mathematical) ontology of disjunction, of the void and the multiple, which expresses the *formal* conditions for events, and specifically for the scientific, artistic and political events that refer philosophical thought to its (Platonic) destiny. I, on the other hand, am concerned with Lacan's articulation of the categories of truth and subjectivity *at the limit* of the history of psychiatry and psychoanalysis, that is, as a reaction to that history and as an effort to redefine its lines, contours and points of connection. This effort takes the form of a *theory* as well as a *technology* of truth. I am also interested in situating this effort in relation to other discourses – philosophy, naturally, but also biology and neurophysiology, ethology, political economy, criminology and penology. Unlike Badiou, I do not situate Lacan in relation to the question of being (or of the Real as what resists, yet is always tangled up in, the symbolic and the imaginary), to that of its articulation to the matheme, or to that of its 'suture' in the poem (Heidegger) or politics (Marx). Unsurprisingly, the concepts I focus on – the norm, the law, aggressiveness, recognition, utility, *jouissance* – differ from those Badiou focuses and elaborates on. I arrive at different conclusions, which are perhaps most visible in Chapters 3 and 4. When I turn to the Lacanian mathemes, it is not to draw up their algebraic list – the mathemes of fantasy ($ ◊ a), of the four discourses (S1, S2, a, $) of sexual difference (∃, ∀, φ(x)), etc. – and reveal the ontological necessity to which they correspond, but, as in Chapter 5, to emphasize their (greater or lesser) usefulness as *schemas* (topological schemas in particular) of basic analytic concepts.[24] And when I engage with Lacan's own confrontation with Marx, it is with a view to extracting the potential of concepts such as the object *a*, or surplus enjoyment (*plus-de-jouir*), for a critique of our own present, defined by a specific socio-economic regime of desire – a notion to which, unlike that of love, Badiou is ultimately not particularly wedded.[25]

1

Denaturalizing Desire

Let me begin with some remarks and observations, which will help situate further how I intend to approach Lacan's work. They are all related to his anti-naturalism in matters related to the unconscious. From the start, we see Lacan bent on excluding from his definitions of desire, terms and suppositions from biology, and separating clearly the field of psychoanalysis from that of natural science. This is a distinctively non-Freudian, if not anti-Freudian move. In his 'Rome Speech', for example, he criticizes a certain reading of Freud's theory of instincts, which consists in reducing them to the nervous reflex arc.[1] There is no question that the theory of the reflex arc, and the question of a possible connection between psychology and neurology, played a role in Freud's writings, even beyond his very early work. Whilst *Project for a Scientific Psychology* (1895) attempted to develop a 'psychology for neurologists', or a theory of the psychic apparatus based on natural science – a hope that its author never relinquished entirely – the ground-breaking *Interpretation of Dreams* (1900) provisionally suspended the task of integrating psychological knowledge into neuroscience. In his transition to a psychoanalytical theory of the psychic events, Freud imported the model of the reflex arc from neurology, which he adapted and complicated: the psychic apparatus can in fact be understood as a cybernetic mechanism *avant la lettre*, that is, as a self-regulated system of internal needs and drives, as well as external stimuli, which seeks to reduce tension and restore an original state of equilibrium.[2] In other words, the mental apparatus contains an essentially self-regulatory tendency towards homeostasis. Lacan's objection – which, it could be argued, Freud himself anticipated with his concepts of the drive and pleasure-gain (*Lustgewinn*) – is that something always stands between our needs and their satisfaction.[3] This 'something' is what Lacan calls desire, especially as manifested in the symbolic order of language, by which he means the gap that separates the signifier and the signified, yet allows them to communicate with one another. This means that, as far as we human beings are concerned, there is no such thing as a pure need, and that every need is always and from the start more than a *pure* need. This also means that every satisfaction of a need is always never quite satisfying, for it is unable to tame the force of desire itself. As a result, Freud's initial homeostatic model needs to be abandoned and replaced by another that distinguishes clearly between instinct and need, on the one hand, and desire on the other.

In the seminar that he delivered the same year as the Rome speech, but this time against a certain naturalist interpretation of Freud's 'Beyond the Pleasure Principle', Lacan seeks to broaden the gap between psychoanalysis on the one hand, and empirical psychology, biology and ethology on the other.[4] He identifies empirical psychology with ethology, that is, with the study of the set of behaviours of the biological individual with its natural environment, and claims that, whilst entirely legitimate as a very circumscribed science, and one that can even reveal important features of the human *qua* animal, it fails to account for the complexities and, more importantly still, the a- or counter-natural tendencies displayed by human beings. There are too many aspects of the human psyche, most notably aggressive, destructive pathologies such as paranoid psychosis, which ethology alone can't explain. I will return to those in the next chapter.

I will begin by exploring two specific distinctions that Lacan emphasizes in his effort to sever the ties between psychoanalysis and the naturalism of psychiatry, psychopathology and the *scientia sexualis* (Sections 1 and 2), before turning to his conception of sexuality, or sexual desire (Section 3).

I. Desire *vs* Need

Where the 'natural philosopher' – or the psychiatrist – talks of instincts, Lacan claims in 'The Instance of the Letter in the Unconscious, or Reason since Freud', the analyst talks of 'desire' as something that is unnatural, or fabricated: a 'montage' and a 'scaffolding', a 'Jeannot' knife, a 'railway system', and, last but not least, a 'language'.[5] The basic difference, he argues, lies in the fact that desires can be appeased but never truly satisfied, and thus cannot be thought of with the model of need in mind.[6] This is because desires are far more complex, even puzzling objects, which partake of an entirely different logic. What separates desire from need is its 'paradoxical, deviant, erratic, eccentric, even scandalous character'.[7] The error of psychiatry lies in its tendency to reduce desire to need, and to think of it as if it were a bodily appetite, the perfectly achievable goal of which is satisfaction, or the pleasurable relief of an unpleasurable physical tension. But human beings do not wish in this way: the satisfaction – in fact, the appeasement (*Befriedigung*, *apaisement*) – of their desire is only momentary, and they can even, and in fact often, be found in the *desire* to be ill or dissatisfied, or to strive confusedly, and at once, towards incompatible goals.

More explicitly than Freud, then, Lacan defines the human subject as a subject of desire, and desire as the basic mechanism of the unconscious, irreducible to need and natural satisfaction. This, he is able to do from two different perspectives, and by drawing on two very different sources.

The first can seem paradoxical in that it is influenced by *Gestalt* psychology, and leads to Lacan's emphasis on the role of images and the Imaginary in the constitution of the ego. Lacan's 'return to Freud' intends first and foremost to emphasize the narcissistic-specular and consequently alienating and derived nature of the ego, together with the impossibility of reducing the subject to those boundaries.[8] In 'On Narcissism: An Introduction', Freud had already emphasized how a baby's psychic development depends upon their being captured by images (both of their mother's body and their own). Lacan reworks this Freudian theme.[9] *Imaginary identification*, he claims, occurs in the subject through the unconscious assumption of an external image in which the subject *recognizes* themselves. Therefore, identification does not imply the mere influencing of an external image on a subject or an imitative relationship between the former and a pre-existing ego: on the contrary, the ego can first be created only because the subject is irremediably lured into the image by the image itself. It is in this sense that Lacan defines imaginary identification as psychically causal: the ego is a psychic agency caused in the subject by their *alienating identification* with a series of external images.

It would seem that Lacan's science of desire relied on the very naturalism he opposed. Indeed, his theory of the 'mirror stage' relies primarily on evidence drawn from various psychological experiments, especially by Henri Wallon and Charlotte Bühler's on child psychology.[10] But he also defends his arguments by referring to Harrison's experiments with pigeons, which demonstrate that the animal's sight of its own image in a mirror is sufficient to unleash ovulation,[11] or to the works of other ethologists such as Köhler (on chimpanzees) and Chauvin (on grasshoppers).[12] The experiments in question show that a child of between six and eighteen months recognizes themselves in the image of their own body as it is reflected in a mirror. Moreover, and unlike what happens with the young chimpanzee, this recognition produces a clearly observable 'jubilation' in the child. The child *recognizes* themselves in the otherness of the specular image: in so doing, they undergo a *redoubling* through which they are able to objectify themselves in the mirror, to identify themselves with an imaginary other. It is important to emphasize, however, that this specular image does not need to be provided by a mirror, or by the actual image of the child: the image of another child of approximately the same age will also be perceived by the subject as a *specular* image. What it means is that the child's relation to themselves, its sense of self, as it were, is a function of its projection, or its externalization (*alienation*) into an other. The child recognizes themselves only through the detour of an other. At the same time, however, this identification is only ever an identification and recognition of themselves, and not of an other as such: it is a narcissistic, ego-based identification, which is the very source of the paranoid-psychotic behaviour that Lacan was interested in from the time of his thesis, and to which I'll return later. In imaginary identification, the child can, and in fact does, see themselves instead, or in place of, the other (*à la place de l'autre*). They take themselves to be other than they are, or they take themselves to be an other, thus negating the otherness of the other, taking the place of the other. What we have, therefore, is a process of recognition that is in fact a double misrecognition (*méconnaissance*): the ego not only 'finds itself' out there, *as* an other, or 'alienated' in an other; it also provides the subject with a false and deceptive impression of unity, in that the ego does not recognize itself *as* alienated. It is no crazier, in other words, to believe oneself to be a king when one is not, as Descartes famously declared in his *Meditations*, than it is to believe oneself to be oneself.[13] The ego makes us believe that we are isolated, solitary spherical beings, deaf and dumb as planets, as Lacan suggests elsewhere.[14]

But why are the child and even the adult captivated by the image of their own body in the first place? This is where Lacan's relation to zoology, ethology and biology comes into play, in a way that cannot be underestimated.

Lacan accepts one of the main tenets of *Gestalt* theory according to which an animal is *instinctively* predisposed to recognize the image of the body of another animal of the same species, and is consequently attracted by it. It is only thanks to *Gestalten* that an animal's sexual reproduction is made possible: reproduction is necessarily associated with the lures of the imaginary: 'In the functioning of pairing mechanisms, ethologists have proved the dominance of the image, which appears in the guise of transitory phenotype through the modification of the external appearance and whose manifestation serves as a signal, of a constructed signal, that is to say a *Gestalt* which sets the reproductive behaviour in motion.'[15] The question, however, is one of knowing whether human instincts, and human sexuality, conform to that model, and function via *Gestalten*. Lacan argues that they do, but in a way that is distorted, and distorted to such an extent that it is impossible to consider human drives as mere natural instincts, thus loosening the grip of the natural instinct on the Freudian concept of *Trieb*. This is where Lacan takes on board Kojève's interpretation of Hegel's *Phenomenology of Spirit* – to which I'll turn shortly – and his specific claim that the break between animal and human life, and thus the transition from nature to culture, is attributable to *desire*. But desire, as we'll see, is essentially a desire to be *recognized* – not as a member of a species, but as *desire*. And this makes all the difference, since the desire to be recognized (as desire) exceeds all possible naturalist explanation, whilst constituting a major pillar of liberal, bourgeois governmentality.

What allows Lacan to claim that forms play a certain role in the constitution of the human ego, but one that is irreducible to the role they play in the rest of the animal kingdom? Put simply, the theory of 'fœtalisation', developed by Lodewijk (or 'Louis') Bolk, according to which the human is, by definition, a *disadapted* animal, and a fragmented or incomplete body.[16] Lacan will continue to turn to Bolk throughout his life, and always in the context of the biological underpinnings of his own theory of the mirror stage. Far from being the result of a particular successful adaptation of the species, Bok claims, the astounding psychical development of the human being, including the emergence of language and culture that it made possible, are the result of a biological deficiency, a *lack*, which we try to compensate for, not just in our early childhood, but *throughout our life*.[17] What characterizes human life at birth is a lack of wholeness or completeness: human beings are born *prematurely*; for many months after they are born, they cannot walk, they lack coordination and balance, and are absolutely dependent on adults to carry out all basic vital tasks. What human babies do demonstrate, however, is a precocious and extremely refined power of vision. It is that power that compensates for their helplessness: the completeness of the subject's body image as reflected in the mirror provides them with a form of unity and wholeness that contrasts with their original incompleteness. The same emphasis on the role of the visual also accounts, as we'll see, for Lacan's early phallocentrism, and by that I mean for his interpretation of the phallus as the symbol around which desire revolves. The mirror stage, Lacan claims, is a remarkably inventive solution to an evolutionary problem. Yet, it is one that introduces another type of problem, and another form of lack: *recognition* – initially of oneself in the mirror – is a dynamic that generates its own problems, indeed its own perversions; and the unification of the subject, precisely to the extent that it takes place through a process of 'alienation', or the recognition of an image that is alien, is fundamentally unstable, and never complete. The specular solution to the problem of human life, then, comes at a cost, which includes the destructive and psychotic tendencies already mentioned. The Oedipus complex is itself introduced as a *deus ex machina*, or as the symbolic solution to the purely imaginary, conflictual, and incestuous relation, which, left to its own devices, would lead to ruin and destruction. In that respect, the moment of the Law, and the articulation of desire around its *recognition*, is *the* civilising instance: the erotic, natural relation itself requires the mediation of a third term, which is the image of harmony generated by the symbolic order, or, as Lacan calls it, the 'Name-of-the-Father'.

At the same time, however, the attraction exercised on the human being qua animal by the *Gestalt* acquires for him a completely different meaning. Animals instinctively 'recognize' other animals, and are thus able to carry out basic vital processes. But they do not 'alienate' themselves in the image. Human beings, by contrast, identify with the specular image in order to make up for their original helplessness. The *organic* insufficiency of the human being is supplemented by an *ideal* imaginary unity. Such is the reason why Lacan identifies the imaginary ego with Freud's 'ideal ego', or *Ideal-Ich*. 'The mirror stage', Lacan remarks, 'is a drama whose internal thrust is precipitated from insufficiency to anticipation'.[18] Anticipation, here, needs to be understood as *alienation* and *projection*, and thus as a form of identity, or ego-ity, in which the otherness of the other is never recognized as such. For that very reason, it is an incomplete and unsatisfactory identification. It is only with the emergence of the various complexes, and the Oedipus complex in particular, that the other will be recognized in their otherness, in what amounts to a change of identification, from projection to introjection, or from the imaginary to the symbolic.

The second impulse, as already suggested, comes from Kojève, whose lectures on Hegel's *Phenomenology of Spirit* Lacan began to attend in 1933, and whose oral style and flair he eventually adopted in his own seminars. The lectures provided him with the means to think of desire beyond the naturalism of instincts and the model of need.[19]

According to Kojève's reading of Hegel, desire becomes truly 'human', 'non natural', or 'non animal' when it intends an object that is itself not natural. All desire, Lacan writes, is desire for 'something else': when we desire, we desire something (or even a person), but only to realize that we desire more than that which we can actually *possess*.[20] Even the child's desire is never linked entirely to the satisfaction of a purely natural tendency. We may behave as if our desire could be fulfilled by the actual enjoyment of an object, or a person, and treat it as a mere need. But it is only to realize that our desire remains intact in the presence of that object. And that's because desire exceeds the sphere of things: its ultimate object is nothing actual. In fact, it is nothing at all, or perhaps nothingness itself. It is not *a* being, to borrow the Heideggerian vocabulary that Kojève himself used in his interpretation of Hegel. But what is this something else (*autre chose*), which I desire? Lacan follows Kojève in his claim that 'the only thing that goes beyond the given reality is Desire itself'.[21] By capitalizing desire, he is suggesting that the only possible object of desire is not the desire for this or that specific, empirical thing (such a desire can only be a *need*), but pure desire, or desire in its very essence, detached from any object: it is the Thing that escapes every actual thing, the Being of every being, or the transcendental object = x behind every object. What we desire – the object of desire – is always lacking, but in a way that is irreducible to the physiological deficiency initially identified. The subject lives and experiences themselves as a subject of desire, and their desire is a lack that no object can ever fill. No empirical object can ever satisfy our desire, for the simple reason that desire is itself without an object, desire of 'nothing that can be named', or 'lack of being' (*manque d'être*).[22] It's precisely this 'transcendental persistence of desire' beyond its phenomenal realizations that accounts for the existence of being, or the fact that there is an object of desire (also referred to as the 'Signifier') in the first place.[23] In Kojève's language: desire is that through which the Human 'transcends' raw, natural Being. Desire is, in fact, transcendence itself. If, at this point, we recall Freud's theory of attachment, or anaclisis, we see a formidable tension looming – in fact, an irreducible misunderstanding that is the source of this drama we call human life. Naturally, this 'pure' desire will always need an object, or a concrete, actual thing on which to attach itself. But that thing will never be able to satisfy or exhaust the *essence* of desire, for the simple reason that desire is nothing other than the *Spaltung* – the split or gap – between need and demand, to which it remains irreducible, yet through which it is articulated: 'Need and demand', Bowie writes, are the 'co-ordinates' of desire, 'but they cannot be co-ordinated'.[24] As a result, desire is

> . . . what is evoked beyond [*au-delà de*] the need that is articulated in it, and it is certainly that of which the subject remains all the more deprived to the extent that the need articulated in the demand is satisfied.
>
> Furthermore the satisfaction of need appears here only as a lure in which the demand for love is crushed . . .[25]

This is fully apparent as early as the oral stage of infancy. For what, Lacan asks, is an oral *demande*, playing on the polysemy of the French word, which refers to a wish or desire, but also a request or plea, as well as a demand or order?[26] Why, a demand to be fed, of course. And yet, to the extent that it is addressed to an Other – to the mother, perhaps – has it not, from the very start, exceeded the *need* to be fed?

From the start, the *demand* to be fed indicates the hidden presence of a desire at the limit of need. From the start, the need is colonized, overdetermined by an unconscious tendency (a desire, a drive). The need may very well be satiated through the demand, but the desire that animates it isn't. Nor can it be. Nor does the subject *want* it to be. For the subject identifies themselves with their desire; indeed, it *is* their desire. In other words, the satisfaction of a demand always leaves something to be desired, something that always transcends the object with which it is temporarily and inadequately identified. And so, what the subject wants, what it desires, is to be recognized *as* desire: 'man's desire finds its meaning in the other's desire, not so much because the other holds the keys to the desired object, as because his first object(ive) [*objet*] is to be recognized by the other'.[27] But the other – the mother, the father – can only respond to that particular demand, namely, the demand to be recognized, with food, which, as a result, is never enough, never quite what we want, and yet, on another level, all we *can* get. The demand, then, has a meaning that's entirely different from, yet always bound up with, the satisfaction of hunger: it is an erotic demand, or the expression of a libidinal quest and request that exceeds the boundaries of need and animality. Therein lies the drama of desire: we long to be loved, recognized, desired. As Bowie puts it again: 'The divided subject, haunted by absence and lack, looks to the other not simply to supply his needs but to pay him the compliment of an unconditional *yes*.'[28] But, Bowies goes on to say, 'the paradox and the perversity to be found in any recourse to persons is that the other to whom the appeal is addressed is never in a position to answer it unconditionally'.[29] A *maybe*, perhaps, a *jaein*, as the Germans would say, but never an unconditional *Yes!* The mother might meet the child's every demand, shower them with gifts, kisses, and treats, she will inevitably reduce them to being a 'subject of need' and an 'object of love'.[30] Yet the child will keep on demanding, keep desiring that which, precisely because it isn't an object, they don't and can't give, namely, their pure love; and they will keep on giving what they don't have. We will do just about anything to satisfy this essentially narcissistic tendency, this drive to see our gaze reflected back in the gaze of the other. We will sacrifice everything, especially the other – the other's alterity, that is – in this struggle for recognition. Inevitably, this *demand* that is not entirely met leads to rivalry, conflict and even murder, as the biblical narrative – in many ways a primal scene of rivalry – of Cain and Abel reveals: whilst desire is the essence of human life, death is the ultimate horizon of desire.[31] Such is the reason why a solution of the most radical kind will be required. In order to nip this struggle in the bud, or not allow it to go all the way, the might of the Law and the power of interdiction will need to be brought in, thus reintroducing the sovereign paradigm within the normative one. What is called for in response to the crisis or drama of the imaginary is the *deus ex machina* of a 'No!' that speaks from on high, the irruption of a moment of transcendence in the immanence of desire; it is the advent of the super-ego and moral conscience.

II. Drives *vs* Instincts

Lacan's critique of naturalism extends to his interpretation of the so-called sexual instincts or drives, and helps loosen the grip of the analytic of sexuality on desire. Naturally, Lacan doesn't deny the existence of sexual instincts. In fact, he sees Freudian psychoanalysis as providing its most elaborate theory. Freud had already done much to show that sexual drives aren't naturally attached to a specific aim or object, and in fact circulate quite freely between objects. In other words, he had revealed the plasticity of human sexuality. But Lacan takes this idea further by insisting that the empirical objects of sexual drives are not only 'variable', but 'entirely indifferent' and thus 'without importance'.[32] And the reason for that indifference is that the objects in question only serve as occasional placeholders for the real object of desire, which is itself always missing in its own place, always there, yet absent – available only *in absentia*. In other words, the plurality of sexual objects is a function not of the plasticity of the sexual drives themselves, as Freud had argued, but of the fleeting and floating nature of the true object of desire, which Lacan distinguishes from the actual, empirical object. Sexual drives merely revolve around their unifying, symbolic structure, which is never visible as such and as a whole. If we understand that, Lacan claims, we understand everything about sexual desire. If human 'instincts' or 'drives' are to that extent violent, if perversion, and even perversity, are innate, it's because every part of the human body – the mouth, lips, anus, fingers, genitals, breasts – are from the very start invested with a force that isn't simply physiological or biological, but imaginary and symbolic. Every organ is – at least potentially – a battlefield on which the struggle for recognition is being fought; every vital function can be turned into an object and vehicle of desire. Once desire is thought to be essentially oriented towards the desire of an other, and understood to be a matter of recognition, as he began to think very early on, the connection between desire and something like a natural instinct has been severed.

Such is the reason why, with Lacan, it can no longer be a question of understanding drives as instincts, why the distance that Freud had begun to introduce between the *Triebe* and life in a purely biological sense is accentuated, and in fact turned into an irreducible gap. Much is at stake here. For Freud, it was of the utmost importance to preserve the fundamental, *natural* drives from a 'cultural' contamination: they belong to nature, they reveal an energetics, and only subsequently make their appearance in the cultural realm through the process of sublimation. The theory of anaclisis was there to remind us of the fact that, however eager they are to demonstrate their independence, the sexual drives piggyback on basic biological needs. As Malcolm Bowie puts it: 'The bodily processes whereby instinctual force is accumulated and discharged need to be protected from the encroachments of culture if they are to maintain their scientific dignity; the drives need to be silent, inscrutable, unavailable to mere talk, if psychoanalysis is ever to rejoin biology in a unified science of man' – as Freud never ceased to hope it would.[33] Not so for Lacan. In his seminar on the four fundamental concepts of psychoanalysis, he goes out of his way to show that Freud himself is very careful to distinguish *der Trieb* from *der Drang* (*la poussée*, the thrust or impulse), which he identifies with a biological or vital tendency to discharge a quantum of energy as a result of a stimulus, such as hunger or thirst.[34] He is equally insistent that Freud does not subordinate the dynamic or economy of the drives to the achievement of a goal (*Ziel*). This, after all, is what sublimation reveals: when sublimated, the drive is inhibited in relation to its goal (*zielgehemmt*); yet it is satisfied.

By translating Freud's *Trieb* as instinct, then, the translators of the Standard Edition had, for Lacan, made it sound much more biological than it actually was. In fact, in many cases, and in ways that are quite fundamental, Freud's use of the term *Trieb* does refer to something like a *natural* instinct. But what matters here is the manner in which Lacan interprets Freud: the term *drive*, and its approximate French equivalent *pulsion*, he claims, are to be preferred. The truth is that *dérive* ('drift') would be a better translation still, Lacan suggests punning, as Bowie puts it, between the Teutonic and Romance languages (*drive-dérive-drift*).[35] *Dérive* is, after all, semantically and etymologically close to *désir* (which is itself very close to *désastre*): both are terms borrowed from the semantics of navigation, and both signal a ship's deviation from its course, whether as a result of a mechanical fault, or the loss of the guiding star (*de-sidus, sidaris*). Both, therefore, suggest a potentially large number of destinations and objects, and dispute the idea of a clear aim, to which the drive would be subordinated. But if such a translation proves unacceptable, and the usual French term *pulsion* is to be retained, one will need to exercise caution. This term, which was created from *impulsion* in the early years of the twentieth century for the specific purposes of translating Freud's *Trieb*, has in ordinary professional usage one clear failing: it suggests that human desire can be divided into a stable set of fundamental types or elements, each of which may be characterized by reference to a similarly stable set of relationships between its bodily source, its aim and the object or objects by which this aim can be satisfied. Freud had begun to isolate such elements – in the form of *Partialtriebe* or 'component drives' – in the first edition of the *Three Essays*. But Lacan wants to downplay the significance of Freud's classificatory work. In fact, his aim is to rewrite the history of desire by wresting it from the naturalism of instincts, and even of drives, and anchoring it into the complex dynamic of the imaginary, the symbolic and the real. Desire is of course subject to fixation, and its relatively fixed forms are perhaps well served by being identified as drives. But the drives only circulate around lack and interdiction, which now occupy centre stage. Where those who allow *Trieb* to be annexed by *Instinkt* are setting up for themselves a safety net, a 'natural' community of interests between wishful human beings and instinct-driven organisms, Lacan returns Freud's readers to the unprotected brink of an original *béance*: 'it is the assumption of castration that creates the lack upon which desire is instituted'.[36] This means that desire comes into being not at the moment when 'source', 'aim' and 'object' enter into alignment, but when an already desiring Other intervenes to say *no*.

III. *Sexual* Desire?

This discussion of sexual drives brings us to the threshold of the next key question: once desire has been reconfigured in that way – away from any *natural* impulse – to what extent is it still sexual? Has desire as the insatiable quest for recognition relegated Freud's idea of libido and his theory of sexuality to a secondary or possibly negligible role? Has Lacan prepared the ground for an exit from the '*dispositif*' or 'analytic' of sexuality, which emerged in the 1840s, and in a way culminated in Freud? Not quite. For there is no doubt that desire attaches itself to sexual objects. Lacan's analytic experience confirms that of Freud: sexuality is on our minds, we can't stop thinking about it, and desire does seem to organize itself in fantasies or imaginary scripts – fetishism, homosexuality, masochism, etc. – through which it constructs its own object. Desire, he claims, is the 'nodal point' or 'montage' through which sexuality connects with the life of the unconscious.[37] The question, then, becomes one of knowing how to reconcile the theory of desire with the clinical experience, how to 'sexualize' desire and present the true object of desire – the Signifier – as an 'erotic' object. One thing is certain, though: the perversions or sexual inclinations in question can no longer be attributed to something like a deviation from a natural sexual instinct (a norm), as was the case for the science of sexuality of the mid to late 1800s. As Lacan famously liked to put it: 'there is no sexual relation', by which he meant: there is no sexual need, no sexual instinct, which, given the right circumstances, can be satisfied, but which, in the wrong circumstances, can also lead to abnormal behaviours. Equally, though, such perversions can't be attributed, or at least solely attributed, to a polymorphously perverse primary narcissism, as Freud himself had claimed.

Far from simply disappearing, then, 'sexuality' is retained as a key problem. At the same time, however, it is displaced and inscribed (at least initially) within the dynamic and dialectic of recognition, the origins of which can be traced back to the works of Rousseau, Adam Smith, and, as I've already briefly indicated, Hegel.[38] It is the latter connection that renders sexuality irreducible to the energetics of instincts – or, as Lacan, having embraced the linguistic turn, puts it in the 1950s – to the play of 'significations'. For the 'montage' of sexuality presupposes the primacy of a 'signifier' or 'transcendental object' that structures and organizes the emergence, distribution and communication of the various empirical objects, or signifiers, which constitute its familiar landscape. Specifically, sexuality presupposes this 'master' (and at the same time 'floating') signifier that is the *phallus*, and which, as the symbolic bearer of social prestige and power, Lacan is careful to distinguish from the penis as an anatomical structure. The term 'phallus' refers to our wish for completeness, and therefore to the experience of something lacking or lost, something missing from this body that I call mine – castration. The phallus is not a physical object, 'like the breast, penis or clitoris', one commentator argues, but a signifier or function designating 'what no one can have but everyone wants: a belief in unity, wholeness, perfect autonomy'.[39] In that respect, adults can use wealth, their career, or their own children, as phallic objects. Why, then, does Lacan identify the object of desire with the phallus, and why does this hyper-masculinist image (or signifier) become the key to any understanding of human sexuality, including that of women? Why, in Bowie's words, this 'monomaniacal refusal to grant signifying power to the female body'? Why, if not as a result of a residual – or perhaps enhanced – phallocentrism (or phallogocentrism), already present in Freud? After all, as Bowie suggests, his model 'could of course be speculatively re-invented from the female point of view without losing its explanatory force: the drama of possession and privation, of absence and presence, of promise and threat, could be retained and perhaps even enhanced if the principals were breast, clitoris, vagina and uterus'.[40] The truth is, Lacan tirelessly suggests that any such transfer of symbolic power to the female would be heresy, and bring the Symbolic order itself to the verge of ruin.[41]

We need to go further still and recognize that Lacan's model of the 1950s is not only phallocentric, but also phallocratic: in its verticality and erection, the phallus is the very image of sovereign power. Ultimately, Lacan privileges the phallus not as the male sexual organ (as the *real* phallus), nor as what is prohibited to the mother by the law of the father – that is, as the phallus that has been symbolically castrated by the law that demands of the mother that she no longer give it to herself through the child, who is the symbolic equivalent of the penis – but as a primitive and primordial 'form', as the fully erect and visible 'phallic *Gestalt*'.[42] It's the erection as such that *signifies*, and that signifies *power*. If it is the 'signifier of power' or the 'master-signifier', it's because it is the very image of force and mastery: like the human body or the stone statue, it stands erect, and is there, visible for all to see, and obey. The phallus is the imaginary 'Master', the literally colossal double in which the child anticipates the mastery of their own body, of their own image as *homo erectus*. It is the majestic statue of the ego, in which the ego recognizes itself as whole. In the imaginary world, where the visible reigns supreme, the phallus wins over any other possible symbolization of the sexual organ. Of what remains hidden – the vagina, the clitoris, the matrix – there can be no symbolic use.[43] The symbol *itself*, by which I mean its logic and mode of operation, is essentially masculine, phallic. If there can be no symbolization of the female sex, Lacan argues, it's because it is 'characterised by an absence, a void, a hole, which makes it less desirable than the male sex, in its provocative character'.[44] Only that which surges forth and up can be symbolized; only that which imposes itself amidst the visible can incarnate Power (especially in the form of the Law). The violence and aggressiveness of the imaginary, narcissistic ego can only be tamed by a more powerful, awesome and cruel instance; it can be governed, but only by the rectorship or directory of the Erect, by the power of the (symbolic) sword. Society is essentially male, and gathered around the phallus, which is the only sexual organ that can be exhibited publicly and, as such, communicated, *symbolized*. It's the only sex of which there can be a theory. In fact, the phallus is theory as such, or the theory of the primacy of *theorein*, that is, of the identity of thinking and seeing.[45]

2

Paranoid Psychosis

Let me now approach the same problem from a more directly clinical standpoint. Lacan's views on desire and sexuality, and his anti-naturalistic stance, make little sense without a prior understanding of his own clinical itinerary. As a psychiatrist, his clinical work initially focused on psychosis, and on paranoid, murderous psychosis in particular. In fact, the first twenty-five years of his career were devoted to paranoid madness, and focused on the phenomenon of aggressiveness: aggressive 'intentions' or 'impulses', hostile thoughts and actions. 'The aggressive tendency', he writes in 1948, 'proves to be fundamental in a certain series of significant personality states, namely, the paranoid and paranoiac psychoses'.[1] Lacan's universe is less that of the 'nervous' patient and the hysterical type, of which the nineteenth and early twentieth century produced many representations,[2] and more that of the aggressive, even cruel type, so clearly visible in the haunting and nightmarish visions of Goya or Hieronymus Bosch, in which bodies are torn apart, mutilated, eviscerated, dismembered and dislocated, as well as in Freud's later writings. Before being a theory or 'science' of desire, then, psychoanalysis is, for Lacan, a way into a specific and central phenomenon, with which he remained concerned throughout much of his life. The phenomenon in question is all the more disturbing because it is constitutive of subjectivity itself and key to understanding our social being. Consequently, Lacan's main problem is to find the causes of that aggressive instinct, and its remedy. Drawing on Freud's own work, he arrives at the conclusion that aggressiveness is a function of a distinctly human capacity, that of identification, and of narcissistic identification in particular. In light of that discovery, his obsession – and contribution – will consist in asking about the conditions under which the perspective of violent, narcissistic identification can be overcome, and give way to a pacified – or *relatively* pacified – social order. Needless to say, this programme goes to the very heart of societal problems with which our liberal order continues to struggle, but precisely by raising anew – that is, away from the theory of interest and motive, as well as that of sexual instincts – the question of the relation of desire to the legal order, to crime and punishment. I will return to this question in the next chapter.

Lacan published his first theoretical article on paranoid psychoses in 1931.[3] He divided them into three types: the paranoid constitution, the delirium of interpretation and the delirium of passion (*délire passionnel*). His teacher, mentor and, according to Lacan himself, 'sole master in psychiatry' and 'the observation of patients',[4] Gaëtan Gatian de Clérambault, had paved the way for his interest in the latter, and in erotomania in particular.[5] According to Clérambault, the erotomaniac is someone who believes they are loved by the person they love platonically, most often a famous figure such as an actor, a writer or a monarch. To the extent that the love is not returned, the erotomaniac can turn against the object of their love, hating them or feeling hated by them. Perhaps more surprisingly, Lacan's article was also inspired by a piece Salvador Dali had published the previous year, in which he introduced his famous technique of 'critical paranoia'.[6] The French psychiatrist was drawn to Dali's account as a way of overcoming the classical psychiatric conception of paranoia, inherited from Descartes, which attributed delirious beliefs to simple errors of judgement.[7] For Dali, paranoia is a hallucination, that is, a delirious interpretation of reality, and thus a creative activity, with its own logic and language. In his own analyses of cases of paranoia, Lacan always paid very close attention to the saying (*dire*) or speech (*parole*) of the paranoiac, which is irreducible to the discourse of the neurotic: the delirium of the psychotic is characterized by a discordance with ordinary language and the creation of neologisms, which carry a weight of their own; they operate like self-referential key-words, which refer not to a recognizable signified, but to signification as such.[8]

In 1931, Lacan published a translation of Freud's 1922 essay 'Some Neurotic Mechanisms in Jealousy, Paranoia and Homosexuality'.[9] In addition to making quite explicit the primary nature of his interest in Freud, Lacan's translation highlights two fundamental features of Freud's analysis. The first concerns the distinction between a 'normal' or neurotic form of jealousy, and a 'delusional' or paranoid one. 'Normal' jealousy is that of the husband who follows his wife to the door of the very bedroom in which she has locked herself up with her lover. But delusional, psychotic jealousy doesn't even require such real references. In fact, as they climb the scales of delusion, the jealous type becomes increasingly convinced by things that are more and more unreal. The second feature concerns Freud's claim (which Lacan will eventually dispute) that paranoia is 'a defence against an unduly strong homosexual impulse'.[10]

Lacan's doctoral thesis, published in 1932, was a natural extension of those early investigations. It focused on the famous case of Marguerite Pantaine, whom Lacan referred to as 'Aimée'.[11] On 18 April 1931, the thirty-eight-year-old woman ambushed a famous actress as she arrived at the theatre where she was to play the main role that evening, and attempted to kill her with a kitchen knife. After her arrest, Marguerite sunk into a period of delirium that lasted several days, during which she explained that, like other actresses and writers such as Sarah Bernhardt and Colette, Huguette Duflos had persecuted her, and provoked her legitimate hatred and assassination attempt. During that time, she also wrote to the Prince of Wales and reiterated her fantasies of persecution. Lacan spent a whole year with Aimée, and constructed a case around her in order to prove his theory of paranoid psychosis and reveal the mechanisms by which unconditional admiration can turn into murder. Although from a modest background, Marguerite was an educated person and aspired to be an actress and writer herself. Lacan saw her action as the result of a complex process of *identification* with her victim, and thus, at the same time, as a desire for *self-punishment*. The other ego, with which she identified, was also a rival, and one that was all the more hated for being admired, all the more violently negated and persecuted for being lovingly incorporated. Ultimately, however, and following Freud's lead, Lacan attributed the process in question to Marguerite's repressed homosexuality and her inability to sublimate it, thus seemingly perpetuating and reinforcing the analytic or hermeneutic grid of sexuality that psychoanalysis itself had inherited from the *scientia sexualis* of the second half of the nineteenth century.[12] As we'll see, the situation will turn out to be more complicated for Lacan, and ultimately revolve around the question of how to understand homosexuality itself. Is it, as Freud thought, a matter of sexuality? Or is it, as Lacan will eventually claim, a matter of (mis)identification and (mis)recognition of *homo*-sexuality?

A year later, Lacan published an article in the surrealist journal *Le Minotaure*, whose founders included A. Masson, A. Breton and G. Bataille. Lacan's article was about a famous criminal case involving the two Papin sisters, who were maids in Le Mans and, up until their heinous crime, 'exemplary' employees.[13] Having slit their employer's and her daughter's throat, the two sisters pulled out their victims' eyes and slashed their bodies furiously, leaving blood and brains all over the house. They then retreated to their bed and waited for the police to arrive. The sinister episode was also followed by a period of delirium on the part of the older sister. Although Lacan's vocabulary was beginning to change, and included a number of terms borrowed from Marx and, more importantly, Hegel, the substance of his diagnosis was the same: he attributed the crime of the Papin sisters to a fit of paranoia, through which the murderers struck down the ideal of the master (the ideal ego), which they carried within themselves, and *identified* with. In so doing, they achieved the self-punishment that they unconsciously desired.

Lacan's interest in the phenomenon of aggressiveness, especially in its paranoid psychotic form, extended well into the 1940s and 1950s. In 1946, he gave a talk at the *Journées psychiatriques* in Bonneval, entitled 'Presentation on Psychical Causality'; and in 1948, he gave another talk on the topic of 'Aggressiveness in Psychoanalysis'.[14] Most significantly perhaps, he devoted his third Seminar (1955–1956) to the question of psychoses, and to President Schreber's Memoirs in particular, from which he extracted an article, published in *Psychanalyse* in 1959.[15]

Lacan's primary interest in paranoid psychosis is important to emphasize, because it defines his initial approach to Freud – one that, from a clinical perspective, privileges violent pathologies over neuroses and hysteria, and, from a meta-psychological standpoint, emphasizes the theory of the ego, and of its genesis through *identification* especially, rather than the theory of sexuality as such. In that respect, Lacan found himself close to Melanie Klein's position, which interprets the ego – or the work carried out in analysis, for that matter – not as the vehicle through which the individual adapts themselves to the demands of an external reality at odds with those of the Id (*ego-psychology*), and learns to controls their drives, but as a process of projective identification involving the construction of themselves through various 'images' (*imagos*).[16] It's also in that context, as I was suggesting in the previous chapter, that Kojève's interpretation of desire in the dialectical relation opposing the figures of the master and the slave in Hegel's *Phenomenology of Spirit,* proved decisive for Lacan. Not before the early 1950s did Lacan begin to recognize another instance of subjectivity, one that is not simply imaginary, but symbolic, and which he identified with the unconscious.[17] But the main reason why Lacan's early work is important to emphasize is because psychoses confronted him with the most destructive, criminal tendencies and drives of human beings – tendencies which, he insists, are both original and irreducible, and, as such, ought to focus the attention of the analyst.[18] This, in turn, means that the focus on psychosis is not regional, to use a phenomenological expression, but goes to the very heart of the problem of desire, and the very essence of psychoanalytic practice.

Lacan defines psychosis precisely as the inability to move beyond the narcissistic-specular (or imaginary) phase, or to overcome this specific form of *Entäusserung* that is *imaginary* alienation, and which he summarizes in Rimbaud's famous claim that 'I is an other' (*Je est un autre*): it is only when the ego does not manage to enter the order of the symbolic, or the unconscious, and so undergoes a radical transformation that (to use Hegel's vocabulary) his *Entäusserung* turns into an *Entfremdung*, into alienation as madness (a mad person, in French, was then known as an *aliéné*). Lacan attributes this failure to what Freud calls *Verwerfung*, a term that Lacan translates as *forclusion* ('foreclosure'). Foreclosure designates the rejection – and not the repression, which accounts for the generation of neuroses – of a constitutive dimension of desire, namely, the fear of castration. The psychotic subject is not, as Freud claims, the subject whose paranoia is a 'defence' against the emergence of a homosexual tendency, but the one who has been *excluded* from the symbolic order of the Oedipal (the Name-of-the-Father) and is unable to reach the symbolizing compromise of repression and neurosis. In the famous case of President Schreber, what fails to be symbolized is his primordial bisexuality, and his feminine function: Schreber is the victim of a delusion that makes him the privileged object of God's love, indeed God's wife, and pregnant with his child. The 'normal' male subject, on the other hand, finds ways of occupying a feminine position in a symbolic relation whilst remaining a man, his virility intact, on the level of the imaginary and the real. Now what is rejected at the symbolic level reappears at the level of the real (not the reality of the external world, but of psychical life), but as something entirely alien, thus forcing the subject to radically revise their categories and reconfigure their world.[19] Unable to establish a symbolic mediation between themselves and what is other than themselves, the psychotic subject introduces another kind of mediation and substitutes the symbolic mediation with a delirious exercise of the imaginary. Now to remain at the level of the imaginary, to refuse the process of symbolization is tantamount to enclosing oneself within an essentially narcissistic desiring economy: narcissism is the night in which all the others are myself, and the Other no longer has a place; it is the mirroring effect in which I recognize the other only to the extent that they are myself, and recognize myself, but only by taking the place of the other. Thus, between the *Je est un autre* of imaginary identification and the *se prendre pour un autre* and *prendre la place de l'autre* of paranoia, there is only a very thin margin, and a difference of degree. The paranoiac is the one who speaks to *themselves* with *their* ego, the one for whom the other *is* themselves. Paranoia is only a form of self-love, of homoeroticism, yet one that is *social* from the start: it is, to use Borch-Jacobsen's expression, a problem of *homo*sexuality, or homo-*sociality*, rather than homo*sexuality*.[20] It is first and foremost a problem of identification and recognition: the paranoid loves (or hates) *themselves* in another subject, yet in a way that is never reciprocated (since the other subject is precisely that, namely, an Other), and so transforms themselves into an aggressive, even murderous being. Paranoia thus includes deliria of persecution ('I love/admire/want to be her' becomes 'she hates me'), jealousy ('she loves him'), erotomania ('she loves me') and megalomania ('I love no one but myself'). If it is a perversion, it is only insofar as it fails to transform and solve the aporias of the initial human complexes of narcissism and jealousy through the Oedipus complex, which signals the emergence of a genuine Other through the recognition of the Law and the symbolic order. That being said, those tendencies never disappear, even in the 'healthy', oedipalized subject. They are constitutive of the human ego, if not of the human subject as such.

Ultimately, then, psychosis presents us with the task of understanding the two fundamental ways in which Lacan interprets Hegel's definition of desire as 'desire of the other'. The first refers to the imaginary, or specular other, that is, the other that is me, or the other that I am. This first type of desire is essentially narcissistic, and has intimate connections with jealousy, and various forms of aggressiveness. If paranoia has its source in jealousy, it's precisely because the object of human interest is the object of the other's desire: from the start, the other is a rival and a competitor, whose desire is my own, or, better said perhaps, whose desire is the object of my own desire. The reign of the imaginary – of narcissistic identification – is essentially exclusive; it is the rule of the 'it's either him or me', of an ego for whom the other is a threat to their own sovereignty. The second and ultimately most important form of identification refers to the ego's relation to a symbolic Other, or an empty signifier, always lacking in its own place, and constitutive of the unconscious as such. It is only with the emergence of the Oedipus complex that the other is eventually recognized as other, in what amounts to a change of identification, from projection to introjection, and from the imaginary to the symbolic. Lacan summarizes this duality in the following passage from his seminar on psychoses:

> The former, the other with a small o, is the imaginary other, the otherness in a mirror image, which makes us dependent upon the

> form of our counterpart [*notre semblable*]. The latter, the absolute Other, is the one we address ourselves to beyond this counterpart, the one we are forced to admit beyond the relation of mirage . . .[21]

It's in the space of that difference, in the space opened up by those two relations, that the difference between 'alienation' – or, more precisely, 'exteriorization' – as the general form of the imaginary and psychotic alienation, is played out: 'We get the impression that it's insofar as he hasn't acquired or has lost this Other that he encounters the purely imaginary other, the fallen and meagre other with whom he is not able to have any relations except relations of frustration'.[22] The 'drama' of subjectivity, in other words, does not end with the constitution of the imaginary ego, which Freud refers to as the ideal ego (*Ideal-Ich*): in fact, the ideal ego needs, as Hegel would say, to 'go under', in order for the ego-ideal (*Ich-Ideal*) to appear, and for the drama and dialectic of love to replace that of narcissism.

3

Crime and Punishment

Bearing in mind those preliminary remarks regarding the origin and focus of Lacanian psychoanalysis, and with a view to locating its significance in relation to both the analytic of sexuality (rooted in a naturalistic and normative, indeed clinical conception of desire, and centred on the distinction between normal and abnormal sexual instincts) and the liberal rationality of crime and punishment (rooted in the concepts of personal motive and self-interest), let me turn to a text by Lacan that has gone largely unnoticed. The text in question, 'Theoretical Introduction to the Functions of Psychoanalysis in Criminology', was delivered to the thirteenth conference of francophone psychoanalysts in May 1950, and written with Michel Cénac, who ended up running against Lacan as head of the French Society of Psychoanalysis (*SFP*) in 1953 – and losing by one vote only.[1] Cénac was a doctor, psychiatrist and forensic expert ('*expert auprès des tribunaux*'). This article is of special interest because it attempts to define the specificity of the contribution of psychoanalysis to the links, established in the nineteenth century, between psychiatry, criminology and the judicial institution. As such, it raises the question of the place of psychoanalysis in the context of the strong connection that emerged in the mid-nineteenth century between the rationality of liberal penology and the *scientia sexualis*: for it is indeed striking to see the extent to which many of the central, normative concepts of the science of sexuality (and of 'sexual perversions' such as homosexuality, fetishism, voyeurism, exhibitionism or sadism) were developed in the context of, and as a response to, famous court cases involving actions and subjects that the central, utilitarian concepts of motive and interest of liberal penology could not explain. In addition, and crucially, Lacan's article raises the question of the connection between the liberal legal order and that of the Law in the symbolic sense.

Psychoanalysis' contribution to criminology predates Lacan and Cénac's article. It began, somewhat modestly, and incompletely, with a lecture that Freud delivered in 1906 at the request of Professor Löffler (Professor of Jurisprudence at the University of Vienna), and before his seminar. First published in the *Archiv für Kriminalanthropologie und Kriminalistik* in 1906, under the revealing title of 'Psychoanalysis and the Ascertaining of Truth in Courts of Law', it is now included in the *Standard Edition of the Complete Psychological Works* under the title 'Psycho-analysis and the Establishment of the Facts in Legal Proceedings' (*Tatbestandsdiagnostik und Psychoanalyse*). In that piece, Freud acknowledges that his work is 'far removed from the practical administration of justice'.[2] But he also notes that, when it comes down to establishing guilt, especially in light of 'the untrustworthiness of statements made by witnesses',[3] on which courts have relied for centuries, the discoveries and the methods of investigation of the emerging science of psychoanalysis may turn out to be of some value. How exactly? By revealing that 'actions which were held to be unmotivated' are in fact strictly determined, thus introducing a key distinction between motive and determination.[4] If those actions seem unmotivated, it's as a result of our inability to look into, and interrogate, their true source as well as their deep psychological mechanisms: instead of acknowledging the reality and efficacy of the unconscious, as well as the singular manner in which it operates, we restrict the sphere of motivations to the conscious sphere, and take for granted the rational agency of interest and utility, which, following Beccaria, liberal criminal law and penology have taken for granted since the eighteenth century. The following passage, from Beccaria's *On Crimes and Punishments*, is exemplary: 'In order that punishment should not be an act of violence perpetrated by one or many upon a private citizen, it is essential that it should be public, speedy, necessary, the minimum possible in the given circumstances, proportionate to the crime, and determined by the law.'[5] In other words, it is now a matter of privileging a reasonable – that is to say, proportionate – penal system for a reasonable – that is to say, self-interested and motivated – population. Insofar as 'the true relation between sovereigns and subjects' has now been 'discovered', proper or *effective* government naturally ought to follow from that newly discovered truth. The truth in question, which Beccaria shared with many philosophers and economists of his time, such as Hume, Condillac and Verri, is that human beings are rational, self-interested pursuers of pleasure.[6] As a result, to govern and, in this instance, punish effectively, means to govern and punish according to those basic mechanisms, and with a view to ensuring '*the greatest happiness shared among the greater number*'.[7] In Beccaria's opinion, the new, *economic* rationality, when applied to the sphere of punishment, had civilizing effects and allowed the sovereign to avoid the barbaric methods and procedures of the past. He sees punishment as 'tyrannous' and thus bad, but also – and unfortunately – unavoidable: it a necessary evil aimed at preventing 'the offender from doing fresh harm to his fellows' and deterring others 'from doing likewise'.[8] It is effective only insofar as it is graduated and measured, and a precise indication of the degree of civilization of a nation.

But psychoanalysis reveals that unconscious wishes and desires can somehow 'motivate' us to act in ways that our own ego or rational self finds entirely objectionable, and even condemns; and psychoanalytic technique can detect or help disclose those often veiled, even hidden motivations and disturbing truths. It does so by paying attention to apparently random details – failures of memory, slips of the tongue, deviations, repetitions or the random association of thoughts – which, taken together, amount to a 'psychical self-betrayal' capable of revealing an otherwise inaccessible truth.[9] As such, psychoanalysis is a distinctive technology of truth, to which I'll return in a moment. Freud never says how the 'hidden secret' of the criminal, which, for obvious reasons, they do not want to share, could be brought about psychoanalytically. In fact, he emphasizes the great difference between the neurotic patient, who wishes to be cured, and thus collaborates with the analyst, and the criminal, who seeks to hide their secret from the criminal investigator or the judge. It is clear, then, that in his article from 1906 at least, Freud does not yet dare believe that criminal anthropology and penology could benefit from this new method of investigation to establish the fundamental motivations, and thus the degree of guilt, of some criminals. Yet, he insists that 'the task of the therapist is the same as that of the examining magistrate', namely, to 'uncover the hidden psychic material' behind certain actions, extract a truth that lies buried and overcome certain resistances in the process. In the end, however, Freud does no more than draw an analogy between the aims and methods of criminal investigations and those of psychoanalysis, without saying how they could converge. Freud's later contacts with jurisprudence were, as the editor of the Standard Edition puts it, 'few and far between'.[10] Not until the publication of Franz Alexander and Hugo Staub's *The Criminal and His Judges* (1929) did the question of psychoanalysis' relevance for criminology and penology receive the attention it deserved – although one could argue that by then Melanie Klein had gone some way towards identifying the roots of the 'criminal tendencies' of human beings in early childhood, and in the sadistic phantasies and fixations associated with the oral and anal stage in particular.[11] In her 1927 article 'Criminal Tendencies in Normal Children', Klein mentions various famous criminal cases (Jack the Ripper, Harmann) as examples of unconscious sadistic wishes accompanied by a strong sense of guilt and dread of, as well as desire for, punishment, which translate into further aggression. She concludes her article by emphasizing the potential value of psychoanalytic work for criminology, whilst admitting that she does not know 'what development these ["normal"] fixations have to undergo in order to make the criminal', and recognizing that 'I have not a great deal of experience to which I can refer in this very interesting and important field of work'.[12] Klein returned to the topic of criminality in a subsequent paper from 1934, also presented at the Medical Section of the British Psychological Society.[13] In that paper, she reiterates her view that 'it is not (as is usually supposed) the weakness or lack of a super-ego, it is not in other words the lack of conscience, but the overpowering strictness of the super-ego, which is responsible for the characteristic behaviour of asocial and criminal persons'.[14] In other words, asocial and criminal tendencies of the sadistic type found in children are a function of the cruel retaliation they dread from their parents as a punishment for the aggressive, often murderous phantasies directed against those parents. The aggression or hate that is most visible in the psychotic (paranoiac) or criminal type is not, however, devoid of love. It is hidden and buried, often in the very object of anxiety and hate, which they seek to destroy. Only in analysis does one reach the deepest conflicts from which those contradictory feelings stem, and thus approach the possibility of their resolution.

By the time Lacan arrived on the scene, then, little had been said by way of psychoanalysis' potential contribution to that field, and much less in relation to the cases of paranoid psychoses Lacan was particularly interested in. In fact, it could be argued that Freud's emphasis on neuroses and psychoneuroses made that debate less likely. The specificity of Lacan's position lies in his belief that the psychoanalytic standpoint on desire is in fact in a privileged position to reveal the very essence of crime, so long as we don't understand the latter in terms of a criminal instinct (following Lombroso), or indeed of a rational, that is, self-interested and a pleasure-driven motive (following Bentham). To illustrate that position, I will focus on two key problems: that of truth, and that of the Law.

The article begins by situating psychoanalysis within the field of the human sciences. Psychoanalysis, Lacan claims elsewhere, is the 'science of desire'.[15] Insofar as it is 'scientific', it would seem that, like criminology, which seeks the truth of the crime (for the police) and of the criminal (from an anthropological point of view),[16] psychoanalysis is a discourse of truth.[17] Elsewhere, Lacan claims that psychoanalysis 'unfolds under the authority of truth [*se réclame de la vérité*]'.[18] But truth in what sense? It would seem that, by identifying psychoanalysis as the science of desire, and connecting it closely with the concept of truth, Lacan is seeking to situate and secure its place within the history of western science. After all, the western 'morphology of knowledge', to use Foucault's terminology, is precisely one that defines itself as a 'system of truth', in which 'truth' is opposed to 'falsehood', and for which science is the expression of an innate *desire* for truth.[19] Nowhere is this connection more clearly formulated than in the opening sentence of Aristotle's *Metaphysics*: 'all men, by nature [*phusei*], desire [*horengontai*] to know [*tou eidenai*]'.[20] It is this fundamental desire or passion for truth, and this ability to *discover* it, which, according to Foucault, defines the western morphology of knowledge – a morphology that finds its literary incarnation in *Oedipus King*. For who is Oedipus? On the one hand, he is the impure, and the cause of the *miasma* or the defilement that afflicts Thebes. As such, he is blind and has no access to truth. But he is also the one who knows, who defeats the Sphinx, and who rules justly. His specific kind of knowledge, or *technè*, and his power as a king, are intertwined: his sovereign legitimacy is derived from his wisdom. Most importantly, though, he is the one who brings together his *desire* to know or find the truth and certain procedures of truth, which circumvent the traditional, oracular procedure, available only to those who have the special gift of 'seeing' the truth, or looking into the future and the past, and incarnated in the figure of the priest Tiresias. Oedipus bypasses those procedures. Instead of consulting the traditional 'master of truth' – in this instance Tiresias – and leaving the revelation of truth to Apollo, instead of truth as divination, then, he introduces what, borrowing the term from the medieval lexicon, Foucault calls an *enquête de pays*, that is, a meticulous, systematic reconstruction of how things actually happened, drawing on facts and witnesses – slaves and shepherds in fact, who have seen what he himself (a king, and the hero who saved Thebes!) was unable to see and know.[21] Those otherwise insignificant characters are now key in establishing a new modality of truth: factual, objective and independent of oath and oracular power. Oedipal truth is one that can be demonstrated, shared and no longer a force to which one is subjected. Is this the desire that Lacan has in mind when he speaks of psychoanalysis as the 'science of desire' and of the 'desire of the analyst'? Is 'truth' – the truth of desire, or of the unconscious – the ultimate object of analysis, and is psychoanalysis knowledge (*savoir*) of that kind? We could easily be forgiven for believing that it is, and for seeing psychoanalysis as embracing the demands of 'veridiction', which underpin the rationality of political economy, penology and psychiatry. And yet, contrary to what Aristotle claims, and Oedipus assumes – and who, in a way, was better placed than him to realise it? – the desire for truth will never exhaust the truth of desire. This is because desire unfolds beyond truth, beyond, that is, any correct proposition, which is mere *adequatio*, or homo-logy, beyond the significations of conscious speech. The truth of desire is the truth that withdraws in what it says, conceals itself in what it utters; it is the truth of the 'id' that dresses up as error. Contrary to the subject as a witness of truth in the juridical sense, which, Lacan notes, the Hebrew *emet* carries, the analytic subject of truth can never tell the *whole* truth, and nothing *but* the truth. 'The whole truth', he says in *Encore* (1972–1973), 'is precisely what cannot be said'.[22] The paradox of the truth of the subject of desire, who is the subject of *jouissance*, and not pleasure, is that its truth can only ever be half-spoken (*mi-dite*). It can only be spoken, and spoken in different ways, but can never be entirely articulated, transparent or univocal. It is, Badiou is right to emphasize, bound up with something 'indiscernible': if everything were discernible in the analytic experience, there would be knowing (*savoir*), but no truth.[23] This specific status of truth in the analytic experience is precisely what distinguishes *le savoir* from *la science*, or scientific knowledge from analytic science. 'The unconscious lies', Lacan writes in his seminar on the ethics of psychoanalysis. 'And this lie', he adds, 'is its way of telling the truth'.[24] As such, the truth of desire is one that cannot be extracted or discovered simply as a result of a (good) will to truth. If it can surface, it is as a result of a certain work or praxis involving the analysand *and* the analyst, the physical presence and position of the latter, and the horizontal position of the former: psychoanalysis requires its own truth techniques and procedures of truth, which never amount to a unified *system* of truth. And that, Lacan claims in Seminar XVI, is the reason why psychoanalysis, whilst indeed the *science* of desire, is not a *savoir*;[25] and why the analyst, whilst not a knowing subject, is a subject 'who is supposed to know'. This distinction overlaps with that between the 'university discourse', for which knowledge is the master signifier, and which, like the master's discourse, is a discourse of authority, and the 'analytic discourse'.[26] The knowledge that Lacan targets in those seminars from the late 1960s, and which is entirely consistent with his critique of utilitarianism from the 1950s, is the kind that has close ties with power – with capitalist power especially – and has taken root in universities, thus subordinating the *question* of knowledge to the imperatives of the market: the current epoch signals the 'absolutisation of the market of knowledge', and the reduction of knowledge to the commodity form. The 'credit-point', known in France as the *unité de valeur*, or unit of value, 'the little piece of paper that they want to issue you with . . . is the sign of what knowledge will progressively become in this market that one calls the University'.[27] And this evolution of knowledge has everything to do with an erosion of truth.

In his lectures at the Collège de France on psychiatric power, Foucault takes his earlier analysis of the system of truth that defines western knowledge one step further.[28] In what he describes as a 'short history of truth', he distinguishes between two types of truth. The first, which he defines as 'apophantic', underpins what we usually refer to as scientific knowledge (*savoir scientifique*). Whilst perhaps buried or hidden, and thus difficult to attain, the truth in question is thought to be accessible in principle and by anyone, so long as they have the right instruments and method, which we are capable of developing. It is thought to be there, from the start, waiting to be discovered. It is the truth of what is, from all eternity as it were. It is the object of a demonstration. To this 'demonstration-truth', or this 'discovery-truth', Foucault opposes the sort of archaic truth he had already analyzed in his first lecture course at the Collège de France, and which he now refers to as the 'event-truth'. This is the sort of truth that belongs to a specific time and place, the truth that happens (*qui arrive*), as opposed to the truth that is always already there. It involves a shock, rather than an inclination. It is the truth that is spoken by the oracle in Delphi, or Tiresias, or the truth of the god that heals in Epidaurus. But it is also the truth that speaks in and through the moment of crisis in Greek, Latin or medieval medicine – a critical moment indeed, in that it designates the point at which life can take a turn for the better or for the worse, requiring the intervention of a doctor. It is a fleeting, flashing truth, a 'lightning-truth', which Foucault opposes to the truth of the sky above the clouds. As a result, it is a truth that needs to be grasped in the moment, or *kairos*. It requires a certain eye, a certain training or the mediation of those whom truth has decided to strike: the prophets, the soothsayers, the innocent, the blind, the madmen, the wise, and, I would argue, the analyst.

Now what's crucial, and most relevant for our discussion of Lacan, is Foucault's further claim that demonstrative truth, which he equates roughly with modern science, derives in fact from truth as ritual or event. Truth in the form of knowledge (*savoir*) is only a region or aspect – indeed one that has become dominant – of truth as event. And what he calls archaeology is precisely the attempt to show how scientific demonstration is in the end nothing other than a 'ritual', and that the so-called universal subject of knowledge is in truth only an individual whose expertise and qualification is based on historically specific procedures and modalities. In other words, archaeology seeks to show how the *discovery* of truth is in fact a specific modality of the *production* of truth. To this aspect we should add that of genealogy, as its reverse and indispensable side. For genealogy shows how truth as knowledge – what Foucault calls processes of veridiction – has colonized and subjugated truth as event, how it has exercised its power over it, and in a way that is probably irreversible. Such a view, of course, helps us understand why Foucault was so reluctant to follow those who define psychoanalysis or Marxism as a science, and why, to those who dismiss psychoanalysis as non-scientific, we should respond by saying that that is precisely its advantage and an opportunity for it to question and problematize the power effects that discourses of truth such as psychiatry and psychopathology have produced and continue to produce. There is no such thing as science as such, or a general idea of science, which could authenticate any form of discourse, so long as it conforms to the norms of science. Science is not an ideal that traverses history and is revealed first in mathematics, then physics, biology, and all the way to Marxism and psychoanalysis. The status and legitimacy of the latter isn't particularly well served by being designated as a science. In fact, and by virtue of their critical function, both Marxism and psychoanalysis are best described as 'counter-sciences', but only if by that we mean counter-sciences within the field of the so-called human sciences, and not the natural sciences, to which they are altogether heterogeneous.[29]

At crucial times, and especially in his later work, Lacan can be seen as contributing to archaeology and genealogy thus understood. By refusing to define psychoanalysis as a *savoir*; by recognizing the place of the analyst as a subject who is *supposed* to know; by pointing to the eventful and productive dimension of truth in the economy of the unconscious; by recognising, finally, and as I'll show in my final chapter, the irreducible historicity of the subject of desire, and its normalization through capitalist normativity, Lacan calls into question the discourse and power of psychiatry, as well as liberal penology and utilitarian readings of Freud. But can we go as far as to say that his discourse and conception of analysis amounts to a return to the *vérité-événement* Foucault speaks of, and that the figure of the analyst is ultimately closer to that of the qualified mediator or the midwife than the psychiatrist? I believe so.[30]

It may be tempting to believe that the 'technique' of psychoanalysis – the analytic cure – isn't altogether different from the technique of confession as it is used in judicial affairs to establish the guilt and responsibility of criminals. Isn't the talking cure a form of 'alethurgy', or a therapy through (mostly involuntary) truth-telling, and psychoanalysis, as Lacan himself suggests, a form of pastoral care aimed at facilitating the conditions under which truth will surface?[31] But this similarity is only superficial. In fact, the truth-telling of psychoanalysis differs from that of the proposition as well as that of confession, and thus from science as well as religion. In their article, Lacan and Cénac clearly distinguish psychoanalysis, and its specific relation to truth, from the strong historical connection which, they believe, binds the sense of truth as ordeal and sworn oath in religious societies, the technique of confession in Christianity, and the practice of torture. I believe they are mistaken in identifying truth as ordeal or oath, on the one hand, and truth as confession and torture, on the other, for the simple reason that the former required the potential belief in, and punishment of, the gods, and involved the existential value of honour, whereas the latter required physical or mental coercion in order to extract a real or fictitious truth. But I believe they are correct in connecting the techniques of confession and torture: both arrive at truth through a process of extraction, and rely on the individual's will to truth (or will to hide the truth). And together, Lacan and Cénac claim, they constitute the two faces of European humanism – a humanism to which, we'll see, Lacan opposes another humanism, rooted in a different sense of truth, itself irreducible to any positivism or naturalism:

> Beginning in religious societies with the ordeal and the test of sworn oath, in which the guilty party is identified by means of

> belief or offers up his fate to God's judgment, probation demands ever more of the individual's involvement in confession as his juridical personality is progressively specified. This is why the entire humanist evolution of Law in Europe—which began with the rediscovery of Roman Law at the University of Bologna and extended to the entire appropriation *[captation]* of justice by royal jurists and the universalization of the notion of the Law of Nations *[Droit des gens]*—is strictly correlative, in time and space, to the spread of torture that also began in Bologna as a means in the probation of a crime. This is a fact whose import people apparently still have not gauged.[32]

But the manner in which truth emerges in the context of analysis is entirely different, and cannot amount to anything like a confession extracted under duress. If there is an equivalent to the truth-telling of psychoanalysis, it is that of 'bearing witness' (*témoignage*) or martyrdom. What we normally call 'disinterested communication', on which the ideal of human knowledge itself is premised, 'is ultimately only failed testimony, that is, something on which everybody is agreed'.[33] The truth-telling of the cure, on the other hand, takes place in the context of what Lacan calls *la parole*, or speech, which he is careful to distinguish from *le langage*. The latter refers to the vehicle of signification – to what, in the *Peri hermeneia*, Aristotle called *logos semantikos* – as well as the locus of truth, at least in the sense of a proposition's ability to say what is actually the case (*logos apophantikos*). But speech is always an *address*, and to speak is always to speak *to* someone. Naturally, and as a consequence, the position of the analyst is different from that of the confessor, the police officer or political commissar, to whom one confesses the truth, precisely insofar as the *parole* of the patient is an address, an unconscious *demand* to be heard, which the analyst is summoned to respond to, without altering its meaning, and thus by following the most rigorous discipline. The analytic ear and testimony replaces the medical gaze and expertise Foucault describes in *Birth of the Clinic*.[34] And that, Lacan claims, is a dimension that is central to the ethics of psychoanalysis – a dimension that, indeed, defines it *as* an ethics, and not simply a clinic. In the analytic context, the ways of truth are thus to be penetrated by following the thin and often interrupted thread of speech. 'I, truth, speak' is the lesson that every analyst learns. And they do so by paying specific attention to the *form* of the speech that is addressed to them. Specifically, they listen to the many 'accidents' that befall speech, the seemingly unimportant 'details' that interrupt or suspend the flow of words: slips of the tongue, *actes manqués*, inexplicable lapses of memory, denials; but also the onslaught of overwhelming emotions that grind the chain of signifiers to a halt, or the sudden appearance of an unsuspected syntagm that causes the discourse to slide. Those are all the 'cries' of a more or less smothered truth; they are the signs of a truth that exceeds the signification of what is actually being said, and reveals itself only 'in bits and pieces' (*par bouts*).[35] They are moments or micro-events of truth. Truth always and only *speaks*. But it only ever half-speaks (*à moitié*). It becomes easier to understand how the following words – Lacan's own – were chosen to open a television programme on his work and life:

> – I always tell the truth: not the whole truth, for that cannot be achieved. It is materially impossible to tell the whole truth: words

> fail us. It's precisely through this impossibility that truth adheres to the real [*tient au réel*].[36]

The 'I' that speaks here is the 'I' of the subject of desire, and not the 'I' of the cogito, or the knowing subject. And that 'I' is also the subject of speech, or *parole*. The subject of truth, then, is not the same as the subject of knowledge, or the knowing subject; and for that very reason the discourse of psychoanalysis – at least in the manner in which Lacan understands it – cannot be simply equated with a discourse of truth: truth is not the object of desire, or that towards which, naturally and from the start, the subject would be inclined. Likewise, truth is not turned towards the subject, with its arms open in anticipation of its arrival. This benevolent conception of knowledge, according to which knowledge is animated by a good will to truth, is precisely that which psychoanalysis questions: if anything, it is despite ourselves that we are subjects of truth; and if the truth of our desire can be revealed, it is at the cost of an alethurgy that, beyond transference, signals the access to a form of self-knowledge that is not given in advance.

The second section of the 1950 article begins by affirming what seems to be all too obvious, namely, that there is no society without laws and prohibitions. In fact, the obviousness of this claim was established by Claude Lévi-Straus in *The Elementary Structures of Kinship*, published the previous year.[37] Prohibitions, and the prohibition of incest in particular, he claims, define the very transition from nature to culture, constitute the irreducible ground on which any society is erected, and the archaic form of Power is established.[38] Freud arrives at the same conclusion in *Totem and Taboo*, albeit from a purely speculative and hypothetical standpoint: the origin of the universal Law, and of sociality itself, is to be found in the primordial (yet 'unreal') crimes of parricide and incest, a trace and repetition of which can be found in the development of every individual unconscious.[39] This means that in committing the crime, the Law itself does not disappear. On the contrary: not only does the murder of the father fail to bring about the *jouissance* (of the mother) that his presence was supposed to prohibit; it actually reinforces the prohibition itself, in that it is now associated with the guilt of the murder, and is thus internalized as the *moral* law. This is the pivotal moment, and the key connection that penology and psychiatry fail to acknowledge: behind every (empirical) law looms the (transcendental) prohibition, and the (ultimately impossible) *jouissance* of transgression. For the criminal – or the primal hord – *identifies* with the very prohibition and law it sought to transgress. This identification follows the primary identification with the Father as the envied and hated rival, and designates the pacific identification with the parental or social prohibition. As a result, any attempt to arrive at an unbridled *jouissance*, and oppose the force of the moral law, will be met with the same opposition, and reassert the rights of an essentially guilty moral conscience. Prohibitions designate the promise of a *jouissance* beyond the mere and necessarily temporary satisfaction of a tendency, or drive. Thus, there can be no *jouissance* without transgression, and much delight is to be found in evil. Yet any transgression is paid for with an increased sense of guilt, which is the very negation of *jouissance* itself.[40] This is what allows Lacan and Cénac to claim that their experience of psychopathology has brought them to the very 'jointure [*joint*] between nature and culture': the crimes of paranoid jealousy and narcissistic identification that caught Lacan's imagination from the very beginning reveal a *crisis* in that jointure itself, a 'blind and tyrannical agency' that is the direct antinomy of the Kantian 'ideal of pure Duty'.[41] They reveal a crisis in the social and moral order, one – and therein lies the essential difference with the liberal rationality of crime and punishment, and the response of psychiatry – that lies not in the transgression of a particular law of the land, attributable to a dysfunction or perversion of a natural instinct, but in transgression itself, that is, in the desire to affirm one's desire *against* the Law, and thus in the perpetuation of the imaginary logic of narcissism. To be sure, crimes are transgressions of the law, and are punished in various ways. The question of who exactly is responsible – the question of punishment – varies throughout history and according to geographies: today, we tend to attribute responsibility to individuals, whereas many 'primitive' societies view transgressions of the law as a collective issue requiring a collective solution. Now it's precisely on this question of responsibility, Lacan and Cénac claim, that psychoanalysis can be of precious use. For it is able to shed light on the nature of what, following the semantics of nineteenth- and early-twentieth-century psychiatry and law, but only to overturn it, Lacan calls 'a force that the subject cannot resist', which leads them to commit a heinous crime.

But it's able to do that precisely insofar as it constitutes a challenge to the liberal, utilitarian order, greater even than the challenged posed by the idea of the natural, sexual instinct:

> Penologists, sure of themselves and even implacable as soon as a utilitarian motivation appeared . . . hesitated when faced with crimes in which instincts surfaced whose nature escaped the utilitarian register within which someone like Bentham developed his ideas.[42]

The hesitation in question is precisely what gave rise to psychiatry's theory of 'criminal' or 'perverse' instincts, and to its focus on sexual instincts in particular.[43] In effect, the utilitarian approach to questions of crime and punishment came under pressure almost from the start, and led liberal penology to turn to psychiatry in the face of crimes that signalled the limit of its own rationality. Far from calling into question normalization as such, though, those other, 'monstrous' or 'abnormal' desires generated a different kind of normativity, and a different discourse of truth, namely, forensic psychiatry and psychopathology, which, very quickly, and as early as the 1840s, established itself as a science of *sexuality*. This is how, from within the rationality of *interest* and motive, characteristic of the economic framing of desire, emerged another rationality of desire, that of the normal and pathological (and often sexual) *instinct*. We need only pay attention to the full title of the work often considered if not the first, at least the most influential study on sexuality, namely Krafft-Ebing's *Psychopathia Sexualis, with Special Reference to Contrary Sexual Instinct: A Medico-legal Study* (1886), to be struck by its intimate connection with the legal and penal system.[44] The problem in question is that of the criminal act for which no reason, motive or interest can be found, without being attributable to the only category that, up until now, had any validity from a legal and penal standpoint, that is, insanity. Before the emergence of this new rationality of crime and punishment in the early nineteenth century, so long as the subject's dementia hadn't been demonstrated, the crime could be punished. But now, a crime can be understood as such only to the extent that it violates a principle of rationality, or a form of efficiency. As a result, more is required: to the extent that the subject is rational, that is, naturally imbued with interests (which, as we'll see in greater detail, can include passions) and spontaneously seeking to maximize their utility, how can actions that are themselves without clear reasons or motives be accounted for, without being attributable to sheer insanity, that is, 'alienation' or 'dementia'? Who or what, which discourse or knowledge, is going to be able to establish the extent to which, and the reasons why, this particular subject can or cannot be punished, and how? Psychiatry moved into that space, which it still occupies today.

But, as the title of section V of Lacan's article suggests, there is no such thing as 'criminal instincts' – no such thing, that is, as 'animal' or aggressive instincts that human reason can tame; or, for that matter, perversions of 'normal' and 'good' natural instincts. In fact, the cruelty and aggressiveness that is displayed in famous criminal cases – from that of Bertrand, the 'vampire of Montparnasse', to that of the Papin sisters – are themselves distinctly human – so human, in fact, that they define human sociality as such: as Baltasar Gracián recognized in his *Criticón*, the natural predators and wild beasts that roam the earth would recoil in horror if they could witness the cruelty human beings inflict on one another.[45] The obstacle on which the rationality of utility stumbles, then, and which continues to define our situation today, Lacan argues further in Seminar VII, is that of Desire insofar as it escapes or exceeds the boundaries of the good and the pleasurable, and embraces a form of pure aggressiveness, or cruelty, which Lacan doesn't hesitate to call 'evil'. As long as what's at issue is the good, Lacan claims, there is no problem, and the principle of utility can apply.[46] But what that principle cannot account for is the problem, indeed the deeply disturbing reality 'of the evil that I desire, and that my neighbor desires' – the evil that consists in '*la jouissance de mon prochain*', and which the work of Sade exemplifies.[47] If those 'instincts' can't be attributed to our own 'animality', or to a mere frustration of our drives (*frustration pulsionnelle*), what can they be attributed to? Only to the very structure of Desire, its fundamental relation to the Law, and the object it posits beyond or behind the Law.

As a result, both the psychiatric (or 'scientific') and utilitarian approaches to crime and punishment, which belong together, prove to be wholly inadequate. In fact, they cover up the *symbolic* truth of the crime itself, and the punishment is, as a result, inevitably inappropriate:

> A civilization whose ideals are ever more *utilitarian*, since it is caught up in the accelerated movement of production, can no longer understand anything about the expiatory signification of punishment. While it may consider punishment useful as a warning to others, it tends to assimilate it into its correctional goal. And this goal imperceptibly changes objects. The ideals of humanism dissolve into the utilitarianism of the group. And since the group that lays down the law is, for social reasons, not at all sure that the foundations of its power are just, it relies on a humanitarianism in which are expressed both the revolt of the exploited and the guilty conscience of the exploiters, to whom the notion of punishment has become equally unbearable. An *ideological antinomy* reflects, here as elsewhere, a *social malaise*. It is now seeking the solution to that malaise in a scientific approach to the problem, that is, in a psychiatric analysis of the criminal to which—in the final analysis of all the measures for preventing crime and guarding against recidivism—what can be called a sanitary conception of penology must be related.[48]

The current rationality of punishment, Lacan and Cénac argue, remains caught up in the productivist and efficiency-based model of liberal governmentality – in the rationality of 'interest' and 'motive', which is also that of Ego-psychology and other forms of psychotherapy – and is, as such, incapable of grasping the essentially symbolic (or 'expiatory') value of punishment. In the liberal era, punishment is considered from the point of view of 'utility' and 'efficiency', and as a merely corrective measure. But psychiatry, as a 'science concerned with assessing the mental health of the criminal type, is equally useless, and objectifying'.[49] By contrast, psychoanalysis is able to reveal the complex dynamic of desire that lies behind the transgression not only of the law of the land, but of normal human behaviour. The (unconscious) truth it is able to uncover is that of a symbolic order, based on a symbolic, primitive crime, that of the father; a symbolic, primitive feeling, that of guilt; and a symbolic, primitive prohibition, that of incest. Furthermore, it claims that most crimes can be traced back to that original desire, that the libidinal economy governs the most violent and aggressive impulses and actions of human beings, and thus that the truth of the crime itself is to be found not in a perversion of the natural, and specifically sexual instinct, as psychiatry had claimed since the 1840s, but in the symbolic *structure* of desire. The Human, Lacan and Cénac claim in their essay, *begins* with the symbolic order of the Law, that is, with a *limit* that both inhibits and delimits my desire.

Thus, actions that, up until then, had had no apparent motive, and had been attributed to the kind of irresistible force, impulse or desire psychiatry described as obscure 'instincts', 'become quite clear when read in light of the oedipal interpretation'.[50] The interpretation in question presupposes that the pathological dimension be seen not in the action itself, but in the symbolic, *unreal* desire it expresses. In other words, behind the real action – a rape, for example – there is a symbolic desire. The psychopath is precisely the one whose life is not governed by the reality that the symbolic structures of society warrant, but by their symbolic appropriation. Furthermore, by introducing the symbolic dimension within criminology, psychoanalysis resists naturalizing the criminal, that is, transforming them into an animal, or a non-human being:

> Psychoanalysis simultaneously resolves a dilemma in criminological theory: in unrealizing crime, it does not dehumanize the criminal.
>
> Moreover, by means of transference, psychoanalysis grants us access to the imaginary world of the criminal, which can open the door to reality *[réel]* for him.[51]

In that way, psychoanalysis is able to present itself as the genuine face of humanism: it is a clinic, yes, but it is also, and perhaps above all, an ethics, and even a politics.[52] As Borch-Jacobsen rightly emphasizes, Lacanian psychoanalysis is a 'therapy of the socius' and a 'medicine of civilization'.[53] Its main concern is to find alternatives to the vicious cycle of imaginary violence, and its goal is to enable the subject to (re) integrate the symbolic social order. From the very beginning, Lacan's aim was to find a remedy to the social evil of paranoid psychosis and narcissism, and to the 'social malaise' that is generated by the current utilitarian approach to crime and punishment. From the start, it presented itself as a solution to both problems, which are really two aspects of the same problem. For if psychosis can be attributed to a 'foreclosure' or 'rejection' of the symbolic at the individual level, and thus as a failure to negotiate the entry into the symbolic, the liberal and utilitarian order is itself in denial of the dimension of the Law, governed as it is by the principles of pleasure, interest and motive.

4

Lacan with Kant

The problem, however, is more complicated. For if a desire for punishment is the real object of the criminal action, beyond any rational calculation, motive or interest, and if the Law is the solution to a problem of narcissistic, even sadistic identification, then we seem to arrive at a moment of reconciliation, however fragile and occasional. If, in other words, the 'true' value of punishment is symbolic or expiatory, and not merely useful or efficient, the legal order in its empirical form can express the reality of the Law in its transcendental form. But if the Law reawakens desire as a desire of transgression and is only a semblance of solution, then we seem to be caught in a vicious circle: for what becomes socially constitutive is not so much the Law as its transgressions, or the Law as what makes transgression possible, desirable, even if and when we obey the Law. This is the context in which we need to understand Lacan's turn to Kant's own interpretation of the *moral* law as the purest expression of the faculty or power of desire (*Begehrungsvermögen*), one that is based not on the fantasy of transgression, but on the will's ability to determine its own freedom by submitting itself to the unconditional power of the law. The moral law, Lacan claims, 'is nothing other than the pure form of desire'.[1] This is a faithful translation of the claim Kant makes in the opening chapter of the *Critique of Practical Reason*, according to which the 'empirical', 'pathological' or 'material' rules that condition our action amount to principles or maxims that define our 'lower power of desire', whereas our 'higher power of desire' necessarily presupposes the existence of formal laws – 'categorical imperatives' – that determine the will *absolutely*, that is, independently of empirical or hypothetical considerations.[2]

The vocabulary of social malaise, ethical crisis and the moral law also underpin Lacan's seminar on the ethics of psychoanalysis. In that seminar, he refers to the idea of crisis, and to a crisis of ethics, to define '*un certain moment de l'homme, qui est celui où nous vivons*', and in relation to which the experience of psychoanalysis – understood as a clinic, but also, and most of all, as an ethics – is 'highly significant'.[3] Interestingly, Lacan traces this 'crisis' back to the eighteenth century, and to the advent of what he calls 'the man of pleasure' – the very 'man' whose emergence corresponds with the birth of utilitarianism, and in relation to which, we could add, we need to think the very idea of the pleasure principle, which Kant and Lacan have done so much to question.[4] Why speak of 'crisis'? Because the 'naturalist emancipation', based on a conception of human nature as driven by pleasure, interest and utility – and most manifest today in the life of the *homo economicus* – has failed entirely to eradicate the human being's relation to the symbolic: the 'man' of today continues to live under a sense of obligation and guilt, and under the authority of the Law, as the criminal cases I have discussed demonstrate. The utilitarian paradigm, when applied to matters of crime and punishment, is regularly proven to be insufficient and inadequate. It would be a mistake, therefore, to believe that our age has become that of pleasure and pure enjoyment – despite, I would say, the efforts of late capitalism to convince us otherwise – and to assume that desire has been freed from the bonds of the Law (by naturalizing the market itself, and presenting it as a field governed by the immutable laws of self-interest and utility). If crimes – especially of the kind that I have mentioned thus far – are of particular interest to the analyst, it's precisely to the extent that they reveal those bonds, and the manner in which they are perceived today. It's in that context that Lacan draws our attention to Kant's moral theory and the ideal of pure Duty, which can be seen as the forgotten corollary of utilitarian ethics, and the normative dimension of the law it introduces: the Kantian moral law is precisely the law that keeps pure enjoyment – the enjoyment of the ultimate object of Desire (*das Ding*) and the Sovereign Good – at a distance, and dissociates absolutely the faculty or power of desire from the very idea of satisfaction, that is, from any affect or motive, any empirical interest or 'pathological' object. But it also, and perhaps more significantly still, dissociates desire from any *jouissance* related to the transgression of the law, in what amounts to a significant break with the Pauline model. Its place is therefore new, and crucial. In fact, from a Lacanian perspective, and in relation to the key problems we have discussed so far – narcissism, aggressiveness and paranoia – it constitutes a breakthrough. But at what cost? And how original is this solution? As we'll see, the moral, Kantian model of desire represents a thorough critique of the utilitarian model, and of the pleasure principle as guiding desire. In addition, it allows Lacan to move away from a conception of desire oriented towards the possession of an actual, empirical object: the fullest expression of desire is not one that is *determined* by the pursuit of any specific object or goal. Nonetheless, there is something – *la Chose*, or *das Ding* – that is irreducible to any specific empirical object, yet unfolds *at* and *as* the very limit of desire. The 'thing' in question does not determine our power of desire as an object or goal, and its lack is not the very source or motivation for our action. But if the ethics are, according to psychoanalysis, ultimately Kantian, can we still speak of a breakthrough? Or is it, as the French would have it, a case of the (psychoanalytic) elephant having given birth to a (transcendental) mouse?

Slavoj Žižek has done much to identify the stakes behind the issue, and reveal the unresolved tensions that traverse Lacan's reading of Kant. In an early text, Žižek seems to criticize Kant, and even Lacan's appreciation of Kant's position, for missing the fact that desire has stepped beyond the pleasure principle already in the interested and pathological desire:

> The problem with Kant is not his moral idealism, his belief that man can act out of pure Duty independently of 'pathological' utilitarian considerations of interests and pleasures, but – quite on the contrary – his ignorance of the fact that a certain 'idealism' (disregard for the 'pathological' considerations) is already at work in the domain of desire . . . And it is precisely at this level that the opposition between pleasure and enjoyment is to be located: a simple illicit love affair without risk concerns mere *pleasure*, whereas an affair which is experienced as a 'challenge to the gallows' – as an act of transgression – procures *enjoyment* . . .[5]

What Kant had failed to see in his very condemnation of interested or pathologically motivated actions in the ethical sphere was precisely the extent to which, through its transgression, the moral law itself generates its own enjoyment, according to a logic that is entirely independent of interest, motive or utility. In other words, there is a *jouissance* beyond pleasure, and it is perhaps that very *jouissance* that we actually seek in pursuing our pleasures. And this, Žižek argues, is precisely what Bataille had so clearly seen, and so obsessively formulated. Commenting on the 'sexual revolution' and the rise of sexual permissiveness, Bataille writes:

> I am not among those who see the neglect of sexual interdictions as a solution. I even think that human potential depends on these interdictions: we could not imagine this potential without these interdictions.[6]

But Bataille's views would not have been possible without Sade, whose characters all seek to attain a state of *jouissance* – a total, unconditional subjection to the cruel laws of Nature, which require *absolute* pleasure, or, better said perhaps, the raising of pleasure to an absolute that is never fulfilled.[7] In his early assessment of Kant, then, Žižek seems to emphasize the view of desire that resonates with a classical, indeed deeply Christian conception of desire, best expressed, perhaps, in the Pauline line according to which 'had it not been for the law, I would not have known what sin was' (Romans 7:7). This transgressive model – it is the prohibition itself that engenders the desire to transgress it – runs deep in our culture, and, as I have already suggested, informs (if only in part) Lacan's own conception of the articulation of desire and the Law. It is the very enjoyment of transgression that Augustine recounts in horror in the famous (and seemingly innocuous) episode of the stolen pears in Book II of

Confessions, and brings him face to face with the reality of 'gratuitous evil'.[8] In a book that is entirely devoted to desire (*libido*), and sexual desire in particular (*concupiscentia*), Augustine insists that the most radical, indeed evil type of desire, is not the sort that involves the pleasures of the flesh, but the sort that reveals the specific thrill that we experience when equalling the Law by transgressing it, without any reason or necessity other than the transgression itself. 'I did not desire to enjoy what I stole', Augustine confesses, 'but only the theft and the sin itself'.[9] And transgression, as I was suggesting, underpins Bataille's entire *œuvre*.

Žižek returns to Lacan's Kantianism in *The Parallax View*.[10] There, he develops a more nuanced – and, I believe, accurate – appreciation of Lacan's reading of Kant. A tension looms within the *Ethics* seminar. Yes, throughout much of the seminar, Lacan continues to interpret the connection between Law and desire along the lines of the Pauline, 'transgressive' model. And yes, there is *jouissance* associated with transgression.[11] But – and rightly so – Lacan also understands the categorical imperative as opening up the sphere of a desire that is absolutely bound to the law, yet altogether beyond the fantasy of transgression and the perverse pleasure it produces. This, however, does not mean that desire gives up on *jouissance* altogether: what Kant calls the moral good, or *das Gute*, and which he is careful to distinguish from *das Wohl*, or well-being, designates a total object or good that is irreducible to any empirical object and more primordial than the chain of signifiers. It is a pure, formal and universal principle of action, and thus one that is not driven by the pursuit of a given or indeed privileged object: an unconditioned, yet entirely conditioning law. As Lacan puts it, 'the form of this law' – the categorical imperative

– 'is also its only substance'.[12] In addition, and as a consequence, the principle in question cannot be *determined* by our faculty of pleasure and pain. The good can even produce a feeling of pain or 'displeasure' (*Unlust*), since it is often at odds with our natural inclinations. Similarly, Lacan rejects the idea that the ethics of psychoanalysis be reduced to a utilitarian calculation of goods. Yet both Kant and Lacan argue for another, perhaps higher form of satisfaction – a real and true *jouissance* that does not work as the cause of the action or the cure, but as a regulative principle or Idea. To be sure, Kant claims, virtue is the supreme (*supremum*) or perfect (*consummatum*) good, insofar as it is determined by nothing other than the moral law, and is free of any empirical or pathological motive. But it does not coincide with the highest good, or with the whole and perfect (*ganze und vollendete*) good, namely, happiness. Virtue, Kant insists, does not make us *actually* happy, but only *worthy* of happiness. The unity of virtue and happiness would no doubt result in 'an enjoyment of life [*Lebensgenuss*]' and a 'self-contentment' [*Selbstzufriedenheit*] of a very specific, higher kind, and one that would not compromise its purely moral nature.[13] Key, here, is the possibility of a *jouissance* that is irreducible to, and lies in fact beyond, both the pleasure principle and the pleasure of transgression. Lacan calls this highest good, or this pure expression of desire beyond any concrete, empirical object, *das Ding*.

The 'Thing' is a purely transcendental principle that has overcome the horizon of lack and frustration, depression and aggression, which determines desire's relation to individual, empirical objects. It is the *jouissance* of the very *form* of desire, freed from any object: the subject desires according to the law, but does not desire the law. Such is the reason why, in a way that is only apparently paradoxical, Lacan will end up claiming that 'nothing other than the superego forces one to enjoy [*jouir*]'.[14] 'Enjoy!' would be the ultimate commandment or categorical imperative, and the purest expression of desire, but on the condition that we understand enjoyment as the enjoyment *of* the impossible, rather than as an impossible enjoyment. The real *is* the impossible beyond the symbolic, or at least what is otherwise than possible. Real desire, or desire as it is expressed in the *jouissance* of the impossible – impossible only from the point of view of the phenomenal world, and actual objects – signals both the culmination of the critique of the principle of utility and a way out of it, whether it is applied to the economy of the unconscious (the pleasure principle), the economy of social relations (the market) or the economy of crime and punishment (the penology of interest and motive). It is resolutely aneconomical. It signals the desire that is in excess of that entire economy, the *jouissance* that no pleasure can touch or intimate. On this particular point, Lacan's reading of Kant resembles the goal that Bataille set for himself in his own critique of political economy: for the struggle of the author of *The Accursed Share* against the 'ridiculous stupidity' (*ridicule énormité*) of utility, his efforts to reveal a desire that would not be 'servile', and find its expression in a purely sacrificial economy of goods, possessions and even the object of one's love, echoes the sovereign good (*souverain bien*) that Lacan finds in Kant. Bataille writes: 'I call sovereign the *jouissance* of possibilities that utility doesn't justify'.[15] Similarly, in his own critique of utilitarianism, Lacan writes: '*Jouissance* is what is of no use [*ce qui ne sert à rien*]'.[16] The major difference, of course, is that Lacan does not follow Bataille down the road of another, alternative political economy, based on sacrifice and *consummation*, excess and expenditure. Or if something is sacrificed (even 'murdered') in the purest expression of desire qua law, it is the realm of pathological inclinations as such, and of love in particular. And this difference comes down to the fact that, ultimately, *jouissance* for Lacan as a reader of Kant is *jouissance* not of possibilities, but of the Thing as impossible. Reversing the Heideggerian definition of death, we could say that *das Ding* is the impossibility of the possibilities of existence, or pure desire.

Such is the reason why, in his 1964 seminar on *The Four Concepts of Psychoanalysis*, Lacan extends his critique to Spinoza: ethics in a Spinozist sense, that is, as the way of desire that leads from servitude to freedom through the intellectual love of God (or 'beatitude'), needs to be superseded so as to give way to the primacy of the moral law as the purest expression of the faculty of desire. The true unfolding of desire is the *sacrifice* of love itself (and even of the love of God) in the subjection to the Law:

> This position is not tenable for us. Experience shows us that Kant is more true, and I have proved that his theory of consciousness, when he writes of practical reason, is sustained only by giving a specification of the moral law which, looked at more closely, is simply desire in its pure state, that very desire that culminates in the sacrifice, strictly speaking, of everything that is the object of love in one's human tenderness—I would say, not only in the rejection of the pathological object, but also in its sacrifice and murder.[17]

Desire requires to be completely and utterly severed from any reference to not only pleasure, but also love, at least in its erotic, pathological and narcissistic form. On this point, Lacan and Levinas agree: the purest expression of desire requires the sacrifice of profane love. And that is the reason why, paradoxically, ethics and evil, Kant's practical philosophy and Sade's cruel characters, are not simply opposed to one another, but are in a relation of absolute proximity. From a purely formal point of view, virtue and evil, morality and crime cannot be dissociated: both express the purest form of desire as unconditional subjection to the law – that of Nature for Sade and that of Reason for Kant. As Nobus puts it, in hearing the voice of Nature, the libertines 'recognize an unequivocal command for them to egotistically seek out the highest form of *jouissance*, which they associate with the perpetration of the ultimate, perfect, transcendental crime'.[18] Their 'fantasy of excess' always comes at the expense of virtue, and especially at the expense of the virtue of the subject who is targeted in the crime:

> In proceeding to realize this fantasy, they relinquish all common feelings of sympathy, respect, compassion, charity, benevolence, kindheartedness, affection, gratitude, shame, guilt and remorse – all those empirical objects and hypothetical imperatives that Kant too would have designated as 'pathological', and therefore as goods to be discarded form practical reason – in order to become both the reliable instruments of Nature's desire, and the invincible incarnations of supreme *jouissance*.[19]

Although the libertines live for *jouissance*, they make sure that nothing 'pathological' stands in their way. They see themselves as the cold, merciless and cruel – yet rational – instrument of Nature, and their crime as the expression of its fundamental laws. In the end, however, we can wonder whether Sade's naturalism is more than the mirror image, and thus the confirmation, of God's laws and love.[20] To be sure, the fervour of Sade's heroes is entirely directed against Christian ethics and values, yet with an insistence and a degree of obsession that reveals those values as the very *raison d'être* of those characters, and the divine order as the ultimately triumphant one. They never seem closer to, and dependent on, the principles they oppose than at the height of their destructive fantasies. As Lacan puts it: Sade's 'apology of crime merely impels him to an oblique admission [*l'aveu détourné*] of the Law. The Supreme Being is restored in the Malefic [*L'Être suprême est restauré dans le Maléfice*]'.[21] The Good is mirrored in Evil, and is formally identical with it.

The elimination of the gap between the supreme or perfect good (that is, virtue) and the positive moral law also entails, one commentator argues, 'the obliteration of the space for inherent transgression which is coextensive with any morality'.[22] If, as Lacan is eager to point out, society is simply impossible without such a space, and in fact coincides with the space of prohibition and transgression, ethics as such signals the pure *form* of desire, and a realm beyond the social order.[23] And if politics (including its system of laws and punishment) is the art of the possible, ethical duty is the demand of the impossible, or the maxim for which what *can* be done can only be derived from what *ought* to be done. In other words, there is a difference in kind and an irreducible gap between the moral law and the political law. And that is the reason why, from a philosophical rather than chronological point of view, Bataille (like Sade) is a pre-modern (or pre-Kantian) thinker: 'he remains stuck in this dialectic of the Law and its transgression, of the prohibitive Law as generating the transgressive desire, which forces him to the debilitating perverse conclusion that one has to install prohibitions in order to be able to enjoy their violation.'[24] He fails to draw the consequences of the Kantian revolution, namely, that '*the absolute excess is that of the Law itself*, rather than that of its transgression. Similarly, Sade attempts to assert *jouissance* (as the *jouissance* of sovereignty) against the law, and in doing so reaffirms it. His characters are animated by a relentless yet ultimately fruitless search for 'the crime of crimes', for an Absolute that, despite the furore with which they seek to obtain it, remains out of reach. Ultimately, and despite their desire to appear sovereign, if not divine, this quest brings the libertines back to their own imperfection, their own (symbolic) humanity; and despite their attempt to realize the ultimate ends of Nature by sacrificing humanity to reach the shore of a promised land – a pure *jouissance* beyond pleasure – they find themselves returning to pleasure, time and again, and as if to their own human, all too human limitations. As Nobus puts it, 'although the libertines' *jouissance* seems unrestricted, it is always to some extent insufficient and always somehow mediocre compared to the supreme state of limitless satisfaction they fantasize about'.[25] Everything happens as if the transgressive way were as much of a dead-end as the illusion of utility, as if the economy of excess, eroticism and sacrifice amounted to a 'crisis' equal to that of the liberal or utilitarian order.

By contrast, the Kantian revolution consists of claims that only the self-legislating subject, that is, the subject whose desire agrees with the formal structure of the law, is free. The freedom in question here – unmotivated, disinterested and disconnected from any pathological object, and from 'the brute subject of pleasure' (*le sujet brut du plaisir*) especially[26] – is abyssal, 'unbearable' even. Nothing is harder than to come face to face with one's desire. Such is the reason why we prefer to fall back on the archaic articulation of desire and the law, which revolves around the dialectic of prohibition and transgression.[27] If it expresses a limit of desire, or desire *qua* limit of life itself, it is one that, for the most part, we want to have nothing to do with, preferring instead to find new masters, new forms of hysteria and objects of desire, a new voluntary servitude and possibly revert to the *jouissance* of transgression, if not the narcissism of love. The life of desire – of a fully realized freedom – is one that is almost unliveable. And that, presumably, is the life of the analyst, and the reason why, ultimately, the only possible outcome of the cure is for the *analysand* to become an analyst. To follow one's desire all the way, to not give up on one's desire (*ne pas céder sur son désir*), would thus mean something radically different from the affirmation of one's infantile, capricious and narcissistic desire. It would mean to follow the path of wisdom. Yet the wisdom in question is paradoxical in that it is defined not by the pursuit of a sovereign good, whatever its content may be, but by the relation to a real yet impossible Thing, which is 'the place [*le lieu*] of *jouissance*'.[28]

But the tension that is introduced in the *Ethics* seminar is not resolved. In the end, we cannot speak of a Kantian solution to the aporia of desire, even if the formalism of the law allows Lacan (and us) to dissociate desire from any empirical lack and object, and reveals the possibility of an enjoyment that is reducible to neither the satisfaction of a mere need (vulgar pleasure) nor the hysterical *jouissance* of transgression. According to Safatle, this attempt to reconcile the Law and *jouissance* through *das Ding*, and its phallic symbolization (or schematization), amounts in fact to a double failure, and one that Lacan himself recognizes.[29] On the one hand, if the Law remains a purely transcendental form that does not prescribe any empirical content, the Law and the Thing can indeed be reconciled, but at a considerable cost: nothing allows us to distinguish between good and evil (or perversion), or Kant and Sade. As Lacan shows in 'Kant with Sade', as well as in Seminar VII, Sade is the reverse side of the Kantian, formalist coin. The Sadean imperative is just as formal and universal, yet produces diametrically opposed results. On the other hand, if the law prescribes specific prohibitions, it betrays its Kantian meaning, and results in a situation in which my desire for the Thing is entirely a function of the prohibition. The subject of desire is thus a neurotic subject, who needs prohibitions in order to transgress them. The law designates the Thing as the place marked by prohibition, as in the case of the mother: it is, Lacan says in Seminar X, insofar as the law prohibits her that she becomes the most desirable object. Desire is then the purely hysterical desire that seeks to destroy the law.

What is the way out, if any? Sublimation seems to be the most obvious (and disappointing) candidate, at least in the context of Seminar VII. Why? Because it consists in 'elevating an object', such as the *dame* in courtly love, 'to the dignity of the Thing'.[30] To be sure, the law does not alter the fact that the subject desires the impossible, and only the impossible, namely, the Thing. But what it does is introduce and regulate the necessary distance between the subject and the Thing. The law preserves the life of desire by rendering impossible the total correspondence with the Thing. It is in the space between the inevitable relation to the Thing, and the impossibility of its realization, that the life of desire unfolds. And the ethical life, according to Lacan, is the life that learns to renounce, or at least postpone indefinitely, this total happiness, which, in truth, would be the end of desire itself, and thus the death of the desiring subject. Sublimation, consequently, appears as the process of regulation of this impossible demand, and the only way forward, the truly ethical life. Through art, or courtly love, or any other cultural mechanism yet to be invented, the subject is able to confront this impossibility without seeking to turn it into an actual object of possession. They are able to transform a transcendental impossibility into an existential possibility, a fleeting Thing into an education and culture of desire.

With Lacan, we saw how psychoanalysis undergoes a radical transformation, in that it extends and radicalizes the denaturalization of desire that had begun to take place in Freud's metapsychology. By refusing to ground the complex economy of desire in the so-called natural sexual instinct or drive, Lacan turns the problem of desire into a problem of – indeed a struggle for – recognition, into a multifaceted relation between the ego and the Other, at the heart of which lies the dynamic of the Law and the Symbolic. At the same time, I stressed the connection that Lacan retains with forensic psychiatry, with the challenges with which it's confronted, and with the manner in which – according to him at least – the turn I explored allows it to meet those challenges. In other words, the Law is present in Lacan both in its institutional, social sense, as well as in its symbolic and ultimately moral sense. Against the backdrop of the history of psychiatry, and the emergence of psychoanalysis, Lacan's writings and teaching can only be seen as an innovative and bold development. But against the backdrop of the history of desire itself, it can only be seen as a classical move and a return to a deeply entrenched connection, that between desire and the Law, whether as prohibition and transgression, or as the moral law, which is itself purely formal. And in the end, it seems that Lacan has little to offer for the life of desire, other than the life of sublimation.

But is this the best desire can do, and hope to achieve? Is the life of sublimation the highest expression of the law of desire, and of desire according to the law? The actual (the empirical) is never, and can never be, the real thing. Is sublimation really the next best thing, the closest we'll get to the real? Is there really no other alternative? Should we seek to disentangle desire from the law, set it free, and construct it outside the law, whilst avoiding falling back into the naturalism of the sexual instincts and drives? Or should we aim altogether to think subjectivity outside what Foucault called the 'historical-transcendental schema' of desire?

Towards the end of the first volume of *History of Sexuality*, when discussing modern state racism, especially in its Nazi form, Foucault assesses the legacy of psychoanalysis. On the one hand, he praises psychoanalysis for having resisted the manner in which, starting in the middle of the nineteenth century, the analytic of sexuality began to overlap and merge with the symbolic of the blood – by then no longer a matter of class, alliances and sacrifice, but of the species – thus facilitating the emergence of scientific racism and eugenics. He says something similar in one of his lectures at the Collège de France (5 February 1975): as a result of its emphasis on the concept of instinct, psychiatry found itself caught between two technologies: that of eugenics, with the problem of heredity, purification of the race and correction of the system of instincts of human beings; and that of psychoanalysis, which is also a system of correction and normalization of the instincts, but of a very different kind. The former, he adds in the lecture of 19 March 1975, led to a general theory of degeneracy and abnormality, and to further technologies aimed at not only curing the abnormal, but also protecting society, the human race and species from all sorts of dangers. It is interesting, in that respect, to note the distance, if not the abyss, separating some of Clérambault's views – whose clinical and theoretical work, as we saw, had been so decisive in shaping Lacan's own approach to psychosis – from those of Lacan himself on the topic of psychiatry and race. In an article from 1910–1911, Gen Doy writes, 'de Clérambault argued for the necessity of partners of alcoholics, the morally corrupt, drug addicts, and the incurably mentally ill to divorce them. The future of the race was important here, he argued: "We must not lose sight of the fact that the psychiatrist is the defender of the Race, and not just the Individual"'.[31] And, when asked by General Lyautey, then Resident-General in French-occupied Morocco, whether he felt the Senegalese troops could be trusted to side with the French against the Arabs, the psychiatrist replied: 'The Negro will always march alongside the European against the Arab as the dog accompanies the man against the wolf and the fox'; this, he added, was because of 'the profound feeling of European superiority'.[32] By contrast, and whilst itself inconceivable outside the emergence and history of biopower, inconceivable, that is, outside the manner in which the life of the human species entered the field of political techniques, psychoanalysis never succumbed to the immunological racism that psychiatry helped forge.[33] This certainly applied to Lacan himself. If anything, Lacan's scepticism towards the vocabulary of instinct, and his sustained effort to wrest the economy and clinic of the unconscious from its naturalistic straightjacket, reinforced this anti-biologistic stance. Of interest, in that regard, is the article that he published in 1947 in praise of the role of English psychiatry during the war, so diametrically opposed to that of its German counterpart.[34] Therein, Foucault writes, lies 'the political honour [*l'honneur politique*] of psychoanalysis'.[35] What made that resistance possible?

A key consequence of the emergence of biopower, Foucault argues, was the growing importance of the play of norms, at the cost of the juridical system of the law. To be more precise: under the liberal, biopolitical paradigm, the law and the institutions it gave rise to are increasingly integrated within a continuum of medical, statistical and economic apparatuses, the functions of which are primarily normative.[36] In that respect, Nazism can be seen as the attempt entirely to subordinate the legal to the normative, that is, to identify the sphere of the political, and of 'right', with that of the norm in a biological sense. The final solution and the systematic politics of eugenics were the purest and most radical (per)version of biopower, that is, the most extreme, and in fact delirious, attempt to protect *life itself*, or the vital instincts and organs of the body politic – now no longer a metaphor, but the political reality itself – from external and internal pathogens, to select those that can maximize the health and chance of survival of the population – now understood as race – and exterminate the others. Nazism, in other words, epitomizes the politics of immunology.[37] The biopolitics of apartheid in South Africa operated within the same paradigm. Now the 'political honour' of psychoanalysis, and the principle of its theoretical and practical opposition to fascism, according to Foucault, consists precisely in having seen in the Law, and not the norm, the key to understanding desire. The distinction between instincts and drives, in the end, would revolve around the distinction between norms and the Law, or between a medical and juridical paradigm. The principle of resistance, then (and strangely), resided in its ability to organize desire around the ancient order of power. The suggestion, then, seems to be that the paradigm of the law can and did serve as a protection against the total (biopolitical) normalization of life, and of desire in particular. On this point, Foucault seems close to Lacan, and in particular to his writings at the junction of psychoanalysis and penology.

On the other hand, whilst understandable, especially given the degree of implication of German psychiatry in Nazi Germany, Foucault's comment may seem surprising. In fact, it might even seem incoherent, or contradictory, given what he says in the very first pages of the same part of volume 1 of *The History of Sexuality*. Everything happens as if, by the time he had arrived at the end of the volume, he had simply forgotten what he said towards the very beginning of Part IV. Indeed, Part IV ('The *Dispositif* of Sexuality') begins with methodological considerations regarding how best to approach the problem of power. It distinguishes between two representations of power, the second of which he recognizes as his own. There is, to begin with, the classical, 'juridico-discursive' representation of power, which revolves around the law. As such, it accounts for the idea that sexuality is repressed (precisely by power as embodied in the law), as well as for the idea, *common in psychoanalysis*, according to which the law is constitutive of desire and of the lack that institutes it. This 'common representation of power' leads to two opposed consequences: if the hold of power on desire is only external, it leads to the promise of a 'liberation'; if, however, the law is constitutive of desire itself, then there is no escape from power, and power constitutes precisely that which we seek to oppose to it.[38] This representation, Foucault adds, is valid not only for power's relation to sex: it's actually much more general and 'its roots go no doubt very deep in the history of the West'.[39] How far and deep exactly, Foucault doesn't say. But he does suggest that the origin of that connection can be found in medieval representations of monarchical power, and in the manner in which European monarchies were in fact systems of right. To this common representation of power, to this system of opposition between the licit and the illicit, the permitted and the forbidden, to this system of prohibition, transgression and punishment, which distributes itself in a binary way between a legislating instance and an obedient subject, Foucault wishes to oppose another image, or what he calls an 'analytic of power' – the very analytic that he sought to expose and criticize throughout much of his life. Its aim is to reveal the many, creative and constantly evolving ways in which power actually works, and which aren't irreducible to the juridical model. His conclusion – one that resonates strongly with the core project of Deleuze and Guattari's *Anti-Oedipus* – is that we need to 'rid ourselves of a juridical and negative representation of power, give up trying to think of it in terms of the law, prohibition, freedom, and sovereignty'.[40] Now the reason why I mention *Anti-Oedipus* is because, whilst subscribing entirely to the project that Foucault lays out in those pages, its target is precisely psychoanalysis as a technology of power that never ceases to plug an essentially productive and positive force, namely, desire, into a system of representation – a 'theatre' – with the same characters, the same plot and scenes, and the same basic mechanism, namely lack, and the Oedipal triangle, repeated time and again, and for eternity. In other words, Deleuze and Guattari's main criticism is that psychoanalysis, precisely to the extent that it reorganizes the mechanics of desire around the transcendent pole of the Law, betrays its own immanence, that is, its own productivity. And therein, they conclude, lies precisely the historical and political 'disgrace [*la honte*] of psychoanalysis'.[41] In other words, what Foucault sees as the political honour of psychoanalysis, namely, Deleuze and Guattari see precisely as its disgrace.

In my fifth and final chapter, I want to argue that, in his work from the late 1960s and early 1970s, Lacan seems to abandon the paradigm of the law altogether, thus largely escaping the (otherwise legitimate) charge levelled at his work by Deleuze and Guattari, but also exceeding the boundaries within which Foucault seems to have contained it. In that late period, Lacan bypasses issues surrounding the 'honour' or 'disgrace' of psychoanalysis, and develops or transforms key concepts that strengthen his historical and critical awareness, especially regarding the modus operandi of desire in the highly normative framework of advanced capitalism, and the master discourses that accompany it.

5

Lacan with Marx

Where does Lacan stand with respect to this debate? Without wanting simply and straightforwardly to align the Lacan of the late 1960s and early 1970s with Foucault's critical genealogy of desire, I will argue that, after Seminar VII, his work became increasingly historical, by which I mean increasingly concerned with situating the significance and value of psychoanalysis in relation to his own present, and in particular in relation to the events of May 1968 and the 'red' decade surrounding them. I will do so by focusing on three key and intertwined concepts, which Lacan either introduces or reworks substantially in that period: the object *a*, *jouissance*, and the Real. Together, they signal a remarkable move away from the clinical-normative *and* juridical-discursive paradigms of desire, towards one that could be described as mathematical-constructive. At the same time, they are remarkable in that they recognize something like a historicity of desire, and raise the question of the historical (or real) conditions under which desire operates today. And this, for Lacan, translates into a series of analyses of the capitalist unconscious, and a rich confrontation with Marxism. In other words, much of Lacan's later work revolves around the historical and political critical power of the discourse of psychoanalysis, especially in the domain of political economy. Such a historical turn, however, does not take place at the expense of structure: as Lacan puts it in Seminar XVI, 'I don't see why the reference to structure [*la référence structurale*] would ignore [*méconnaîtrait*] the historical dimension'.[1] It is, he says, a matter of recognizing the historicity of structure, or the manner in which structure unfolds historically. At the same time, it is a matter of understanding the way in which history does not call structure into question so much as reconfigures it, or distributes its coordinates according to a specific position. This point brings us back to my Introduction, in which I situated the question of the conditions of desire *between* genesis and structure, and in relation to the status of the Real. As a self-confessed structuralist, whose own conception of structure was rooted in Saussure's linguistics as mediated and transformed by Lévi-Strauss' anthropology, Lacan was bound to find himself embroiled in the polemics that opposed the partisans of structure and those of genesis in France in the late 1950s and 1960s, and which affected every discipline, from biology to mathematics, philosophy, the study of religions, psychology and psychoanalysis. The historical significance and structuring dimension of this opposition, which some tried to question and overcome, was fully revealed in the 1959 Colloque de Cerisy, *Entretiens sur les notions de genèse et de structure*.[2] But it continued to shape debates throughout the 1960s. Lacan's topological turn needs to be understood in that light.

As we saw, much of Seminar VII revolved around the concept of *das Ding*, or *la Chose*, which was bound up with that of *jouissance*: the Thing is the true place of *jouissance*. I say true, because we saw how *jouissance*, as designating a horizon of experience beyond pleasure and utility, is found in the fantasy of transgression and mastery (and often associated with bodily pleasures), as well as in the subjection to the Law, and thus as a *jouissance* of the Law.[3] Whilst *das Ding* is the true place of *jouissance*, it also designates – as the unity of virtue and happiness – the *jouissance* of the impossible, and the experience of the real *qua* impossible. To be sure, the Thing is the force that attracts desire. But it is also an attractor desire can never coincide with. It signals a limit and a reality beyond symbolization. It is worth noting that whilst the concept of *jouissance* becomes increasingly important in Lacan's later work, and is arguably its central concept, that of the Thing seems to vanish.[4] Why? What is the problem with the Thing, such that it can no longer sustain, or no longer sustain on its own, *jouissance* as the horizon of desire beyond the pleasure principle? Or, better said perhaps, is *jouissance* itself, as essentially different from pleasure, only impossible?[5]

I. Preliminary Remarks

1. It is worth emphasizing that, in Lacan's later work, the Thing does not so much disappear as splinter into a multiplicity of discrete objects ('objects *a*') which, far from attracting and guiding desire as a whole, as *das Ding* did, merely provoke or cause it.[6] This means that the economy of desire is no longer defined in relation to the Law and the Thing, but by the fragmentation and dissemination of the latter into a manifold of objects that operate as substitutes, indeed supplements of *jouissance*.[7] By calling them supplements, and referring to the concept of dissemination, I wish to draw on the strong philosophical sense of those words, which we have learned from Derrida: a

supplement reveals and compensates for a deficiency – a lack of self-identity and self-presence – that is constitutive of a given object or system; dissemination signals the absence of final synthesis or closure that is inherent in discourse. In Lacan, objects *a* correspond to a double logic of supplementarity: on the one hand, they postpone indefinitely the moment of *jouissance*, and emphasize its loss; on the other hand, they compensate for the *loss* of *jouissance*, or plug the hole left by its absence. Whereas the Thing designates the gathering or unity of the subject, the One that unfolds *at* and *as* the limit of desire, or being as self-presence and self-identity, the object *a* signals another, opposed limit: a process of detachment and isolation, extraction and selection from a chain of signifiers. The process in question isolates a part of a whole – initially a body part – and it is through this process that it becomes an object. Thus, the infant detaches the breast from the mother's body, and establishes a connection between that object and its own mouth. At the same time, insofar as the child identified with the mother, this detachment is also a detachment from itself, a sundering within the subject itself, a loss of unity. This means that the subject (dis)constitutes itself through this process of objectification. The object thus serves as a limit, fold or articulation between inside and outside, loss and *jouissance*, the subject and the Other. Whether as partial (Klein) or transitional (Winnicott), it takes on a life of its own and becomes an object of desire.

The objects of adult sexuality are as partial as the lost objects of infantile sexuality, and are only substitutes for such lost objects:

> This is the hollow, the gap that no doubt a number of objects initially come and fill—objects that, in some way, are adapted in

> advance, designed to be as stoppers. This is no doubt where a classical analytic practice stops, with its emphasis upon these various terms, oral, anal, scopic, not to mention vocal.[8]

What is registered in, say, the oral drive, is the lost and missing maternal breast. More revealing still is the *gaze* as the object *a* of the scopic drive, which illustrates the fleeting character of the object of the drive, as well as its irreducible difference from any empirical object. The gaze, which the scopic drive seeks to grasp, is essentially different from the eye that sustains it, precisely by virtue of its invisible, unrepresentable character. It constantly reactivates the scopic drive in its attempt to anchor its fleeting manifestation in various empirical objects. In short, it exemplifies the object *a* as 'the object that is eternally missing'.[9] In any event, whatever is registered in the object of the drive is registered as a loss (*une perte*), a deficiency (*défaut*), a failure (*échec*). The function of the object *a* is indeed to register this loss, to schematize an Idea, the Thing, through the multiplication of empirical objects: 'And it is in the place of this loss introduced by repetition that we see the function of the lost object emerge, of what I am calling the *a*'.[10] The object small a is a *trace*, and the mark of an essentially nostalgic subject, who revels in the 'ruinous' *jouissance* of loss.[11] Loss is the condition of repetition, yet repetition only recovers the loss of *jouissance*. *Jouissance* exists only in repetition, yet repetition emphasizes the loss of *jouissance*. Properly speaking, then, *jouissance* exists only as a *plus-de-jouir*, as a supplement and the expression of an aporetic desire. The object that marks this logic is ontologically distinctive in that it has an empirical as well as a transcendental side, and remains undecided between a given empirical object and *das*

Ding. It is the experience and repetition of the Thing, but only as and through loss; the next best thing to the thing itself, but not quite the thing. As such, it is the mark of a split or cracked subject, and equally of a subject that refuses to accept this loss, to let go of the Thing altogether. Following Freud, yet in a way that the father of psychoanalysis never quite thematized, what Lacan is attempting to capture in the concept of the *plus-de-jouir*, especially in relation to that of repetition, is the double, supplementary dimension of the compulsion to repeat: on the one hand, repetition always involves a loss, and even generates the loss through the repetition; on the other hand, the repetition compensates for the loss, opens up an indefinite horizon of repetition, such that, at the limit, the lost object might eventually be recovered. The logic of repetition is one of surplus: loss generates excess. The 'plus' in *plus-de-jouir* signals a 'no more' (as in *il n'y a plus de place* or *il n'y a plus d'argent*) and a loss. Its fate is bound up with an irreducible *manque-à-jouir*. Modelled after the French *manque à gagner*, Lacan's concept designates a shortfall or missed opportunity to realize a gain *and* a surplus. But the *plus-de-jouir* also signals an excess or a surplus, and, beyond that, an injunction or command (*plus de jouir, plus*!), a new categorical imperative based on the renunciation of true *jouissance*: a frenetic *jouissance* of the proliferation of objects *a*. It is at once the mark of an impossible *jouissance*, and that by which something of *jouissance* is returned to the subject.

In a move that signals the translation of the transcendental (or quasi-transcendental) into the historical, of ontogenesis into phylogenesis, Lacan's further claim is that, under the historically defined capitalist mode of production and consumption, the object *a* becomes dominant as a commodity and takes on a life of its own: it is reducible neither to an unattainable transcendent Thing (as in the troubadour's fetishization of the Lady) nor to an immanent *agalma* (as in Alcibiades's fetishization of Socrates as a godlike figure in Plato's *Symposium*).[12] Commodities, and the commodification of the space of desire, are the current historical realization of this logic of atomization and proliferation of desire without closure. Having said that, and in light of the most recent wave of nationalism and reactionary politics that has swept across Europe and the United States, it would seem that the spectre of the Thing has returned, in the form of a ruinous *jouissance* of the loss of the *xenos* and the nation, of Empire, if not of (Christian) values and white power. I will return to capitalist *jouissance* and desire in the second part of this chapter.

2. Unsurprisingly, Lacan's renewed conception of *jouissance* leads him to reassess the fundamental meaning of the Freudian compulsion of repetition (*Wiederholungszwang*), and its connection with the death drive (*Todestrieb*). *Jouissance*, Lacan claims in Seminar XVII (14 January 1970), is the mechanism or phenomenon that underpins repetition in the Freudian sense, that is, the – *prima facie* incomprehensible – unconscious compulsion to repeat conflicts, unpleasant and even traumatic events. By *jouissance*, he has in mind the force or impulse that overrides 'normal' life itself, understood as a state of homeostasis or harmony between the *Umwelt* and the *Innenwelt*, which Freud identifies with our feeling of appeasement and therefore pleasure: 'The living being who functions normally purrs with pleasure [*l'être vivant qui tourne normalement ronronne dans le plaisir*]'.[13] If *jouissance* is remarkable, Lacan goes on to say, it is as a result of its ability to introduce a deviation from that normal state,

in excess of pleasure. But this deviation is not, or at least no longer to be confused with a transgression, that is, a sudden irruption within, and interruption of, a field prohibited by virtue of the self-regulation of the vital apparatuses: 'we don't transgress anything. To sneak through is not to transgress [*on ne transgresse rien. Se faufiler n'est pas transgresser*]'.[14] The sneaky *jouissance* in question is not transgressive, and thus not opposed to the Law. But it is not reducible to the mere energetics of life either, and specifically to the value of entropy as signalling a loss of energy and increase in disorder, which in turn requires more work, or the production of surplus energy. This other force or drive, which runs counter-stream to that of life, is death: 'the path toward death is nothing other than what we call *jouissance*'.[15] But death is itself outside life, inorganic. In other words, *jouissance* points to the existence of a drive beyond equilibrium, one oriented towards the inanimate and lifelessness. This means, crucially, that the life of the psyche is not simply a matter of instinct, and that repetition does not designate simply, or even primarily, the cycle of need and satisfaction that characterizes biological life. It is not even life in the expanded sense, that is, as including the drive towards self-preservation (*Ichtrieb*) *and* pleasure (*Lust-Ich, Sexualtrieb*), which Freud had distinguished in *Triebe und Triebschicksale* (1915), but subsumed under the concepts of Life and Eros in *Beyond the Pleasure Principle*. The economy of the unconscious, and thus of desire, is also governed by a cycle that coincides with the disappearance of biological life, and the return to the inanimate. Such is the reason why Lacan defines *jouissance* as essentially masochistic (and masochism – unlike sadism, which seeks to cause shame in the victim – as an experience of *jouissance*): it is the enjoyment of the inanimate, or the otherwise than animate. This is also the reason why, in Seminar XVI, he claims that psychoanalysis reveals the true colours of *jouissance*: whereas Stoicism, Epicureanism and the various doctrines of pleasure paint a world in black and white, with the psychoanalytic experience, and that of repetition in particular, we begin to see things in colour. *Jouissance* is reducible to neither pleasure nor pain, and can in fact explain both. It is prior to, if not the very a priori of, desire, in excess of the immanence of life as well as the transcendence of the Law, of biological as well as symbolic normativity. It is irreducible to phallic or sexual *jouissance*, which is never complete, always *en reste de jouissance*; it is even the 'obstacle owing to which man does not come [*n'arrive pas*], I would say, to enjoy [*jouir de*] the body of the woman, precisely because what he enjoys is the *jouissance* of the organ'.[16] She withholds something, generates a remainder (*reste*), and this in such a way that, like Achilles in his attempt to catch up with the tortoise, he may very well step ahead of her, but never manages to meet up with her: there is, after all, no such thing as a sexual *relationship*. Equally, *jouissance* accounts for the origin of right itself, independently of any transgressive or conformist relation to the law. As Lacan puts it in *Encore*: 'This is where the essence of right [*le droit*] resides – to allocate [*répartir*], distribute [*distribuer*], retribute [*rétribuer*] *jouissance* [*ce qu'il en est de la jouissance*]'.[17] Right, in other words, is concerned with the question of who enjoys what, how, how far and for how long, etc. And it is expressed as a matter not of transgression, or indeed of the *jouissance* associated with a certain subjection to its sovereign, uncompromising, categorical imperative, and the ideal of a supreme good, but of a negotiation, a distribution, an allocation of a range of objects, to which corresponds a limited enjoyment. At the same time, by anchoring *jouissance* in a juridical context, Lacan loosens further its connection with sexuality, and with the normativity of the *scientia sexualis*: So yes, *jouissance* signals a horizon beyond sexuality and the pleasure principle, but also opens up perspectives beyond the (Kantian) reign of the Law and the Thing.

3. Lacan's later work also coincides with a flourishing of topological models applied to non-spherical objects, or objects without a centre, and to the world of knots in particular.[18] This is no coincidence: as Lacan tries to undo the initial knot of desire, of its articulation to the norm, to the Law and the Thing, he finds in nodology inventive ways of thinking the manner in which desire is constructed, deconstructed and reconstructed, assembled and reassembled. The knot becomes the more adequate and flexible schema through which Lacan thinks the inner articulations of the subject of desire (*jouissance*, object *a*, the real). How, then, can we reconcile Lacan's increasing historical concern with his growing interest in topology? '*Qu'en est-il du désir qui soutient, de la façon la plus cachée, le discours qui en est apparemment le plus abstrait, disons, le discours mathématique?*'[19] Whilst abstract, mathematics and topological models in particular are real in the structural sense: they formalize the many ways in which surfaces can transform, and generate new forms; the way in which space is not reducible to extension, but is constituted by relations and intensive properties. Let me illustrate this point by turning once again to the status of objects *a*, and bearing in mind that the three key concepts I'll be focusing on in this chapter can't be isolated from one another. Objects *a* are discontinuous and characterized by the fact that they appear and disappear suddenly, and are not organized according to a Newtonian, gravitational model: they don't revolve around a central Object. Instead, they partake of what one commentator describes as a

'microphysics', one that Lacan compares with the work of analysis itself, and a mathematical constructivism.[20] A precedent, which Lacan does not acknowledge, can be found in Freud. Where Freud's *Entwurf einer Psychologie* (1895), which Lacan privileges in Seminar VII, can indeed be read through the Copernican (or Newtonian) schema of the Thing, *Kronstruktionen in der Analyse* (1937), which Lacan comments on only in *Seminar I*, but could be said to orient much of his later thought, provides a model adequate to think the object *a*. In that late text, and in marked contrast with his early investigations on the primal scene, envisaged as a kind of search for origins, Freud shows how the history of the subject is radically forgotten, including by himself, and that it can't be as simple as recovering it as it *actually* unfolded. Instead – and that is the purpose of analysis – it is a matter of 'reconstructing' it, yet in a way that does not seek to imitate something that is meant to have happened, and with which the construction would coincide. This is the point at which interpretation, often thought – by Freud included – to designate the nature of analytic technique, proves insufficient:

> If, in accounts of analytic technique, so little is said about 'constructions,' that is because 'interpretations' and their effects are spoken of instead. But I think that 'construction' is by far the more appropriate description.[21]

To be sure, for much of the essay reconstruction refers to the work of the analyst: unlike the patient, who recovers lost – 'repressed' – memories through fragments of these memories in dreams, free association or repetitions of the affects belonging to the repressed material in certain actions, the analyst could not possibly remember such fragments. Instead, and not unlike an archaeologist, they construct or reconstruct the past of the analysand by 'supplementing and combining' its surviving remains.[22] A picture thus emerges, the truth or correctness of which can never be entirely ascertained, and certainly not through either the acquiescence or resistance of the patient. Yet, in his concluding remarks, Freud turns to the constructive work of the patients themselves, and opens up fruitful lines of investigation, which Lacan seems to have taken up in his own way. He remarks how, on a number of occasions and when presented with a particularly apt construction, patients have lively recollections not of the main event recounted in the construction, but of specific details surrounding it, such as the faces of the people involved in the construction, or the disposition of furniture, on the subject of which the construction had no possibility of any knowledge. Now these recollections could be dismissed as hallucinations. Yet what are hallucinations? They are, Freud claims, the return of something painful that has been experienced in infancy and then forgotten – something 'that now forces its way into consciousness, probably distorted and displaced owing to the operation of forces that are opposed to this return'.[23] There is, therefore, 'a fragment of *historical truth*' and, I would add, a form of truth *as* fragment, in hallucinations, delusions and madness. The delusions of patients are themselves 'the equivalents of the constructions' that the analyst builds in the course of an analytic treatment.[24] Both attempt to liberate a fragment of historical truth from its distortions and its attachment to a present, rejected reality. To be sure, psychotics 'can do no more than replace the fragment of a reality that is being disavowed in the present by another fragment that has already been disavowed in the remote past'.

As such, psychosis cannot serve as a model of reconstruction. But the emphasis on fragments is what matters here, and justifies this remarkable proximity between the *method* of the analysts and the *truth* of the patient's experience.

It is odd, Cléro concludes, that given the significance of the concepts of construction and reconstruction in Lacan, he cites Freud's seminal text only once.[25] At the same time, it is clear that the concept of the object *a* allows Lacan to extend this Freudian insight to the reality of the unconscious as a whole: the object of desire is not one that we simply conform to, or intend. It is one that we *construct*, and perhaps even produce. Reality is no longer that against which the representations (or fantasies) of the unconscious are measured, but the *effect* of the unconscious itself, which is now seen as immediately and intrinsically productive. Desire is no longer defined in terms of intentionality, and the pursuit of an elusive (for purely transcendental) object. It is now seen as constructive, if not constructivist. The reality of desire is now one in which objects are invested and constructed, and no longer simply as placeholders for, and always falling short of, the Thing and its (impossible) *jouissance*. The link with interpretation begins to loosen, and psychoanalysis – as a theory as well as a practice – becomes less of a hermeneutics and more of a constructivism.

II. Surplus Enjoyment: Lacan with Marx

The most explicit connection of *jouissance* as *plus-de-jouir*, however, is with Marx's concept of surplus value.

Before I turn to the deep affinity between the concept of surplus value and that of *plus-de-jouir*, or surplus enjoyment, and as a way of introducing it yet differently, I want to note that, on several occasions in that period, Lacan returns to the so-called master-slave dialectic in Hegel's *Phenomenology*, which he also describes as a dialectic of *jouissance* and, starting in Seminar XVII, equates with 'the master's discourse'. What characterizes this dialectic, he claims, and applies to *jouissance* as a whole, is that, contrary to popular belief, it stages not the triumph, but the renunciation or sacrifice of *jouissance*. It does so in relation to the master as well as the servant. The master, in risking his life and staring death in the eye, relinquishes the enjoyment of his life and body. The servant, who initially enjoys his bodily existence by virtue of having chosen life, is eventually forced into a life of toil. In both cases, the renunciation involves a frustration: for the master, who abandons enjoyment to the servant; for the servant who – and this is the point at which the Marxist, rather than strictly Hegelian move is introduced – is robbed of the true value of his or her labour. This means that the renunciation of *jouissance* does not lead to a moment of resolution, or something like a letting-go of *jouissance*, but is affirmed negatively, as a *jouissance* that is inaccessible, barred. And that is the origin of what Lacan means by the *plus-de-jouir*: a *manque-à-jouir* that leads to a supplement of enjoyment. This situation is also the point of departure for any assessment of the social relations of capitalism (as well as, one imagines, of any relation of power involving a similar situation, such as that between the white and/or male signifier and the colonized and/or female subject), and this means for the manner in which the work of the subject of capitalism is appropriated by the capitalist in the form of surplus value.

Let me now turn more specifically to the Marxian background of this concept, which Lacan develops most explicitly in Seminar XVI (*D'un Autre à l'autre*). He identifies the *plus-de-jouir* (*Mehrlust*, as he likes to translate it into German, a better translation of which would be *Mehrgenuss*) with Marx's concept of surplus value (*Mehrwert*). They are, he says, cut 'in the same cloth'.[26] This means that their connection is not one of analogy, or vague resemblance, but unity. In his long interview with the Belgian radio from 1970, he says: '*Mehrwert* is actually *Marxlust*, Marx's *plus-de-jouir*'.[27] To be clear: whilst the *plus-de-jouir* is modelled after the concept of surplus value, it also sheds new light on the Marxist concept and accounts for its necessity outside a strictly socio-economic problematic. This is key, because it inscribes dialectical materialism within the broader analytic of desire, and the critique of political economy within libidinal economy. At the same time, it introduces a new dimension within the analytic of desire, one that renders possible, and indeed calls for, an *historical* critique of libidinal economy. To put it succinctly: this development signals the fragmentation of the Thing into a multiplicity of objects (objects *a*), which are the *supplements* of *jouissance*; a surplus enjoyment, then, which stands for both the impossibility of *jouissance* and its insistence. And within this (now topological) structure, capitalism grows and thrives. Within this *manque-à-jouir*, and its originary supplement, use value is realized as surplus value through social relations of exploitation.

The first thing to note is that the *plus-de-jouir* accounts for the *production* of the object *a*.[28] It therefore points in the direction of the conditions of production or emergence of that object, which Lacan describes as the 'cause' of desire, or of a certain type of desire. The second thing to note and recall is that, like labour, the *plus-de-jouir* is a function or effect not of *jouissance*, but of the renunciation of *jouissance*, and it is in the space of that renunciation that the object *a* finds its place. So, we have the following logical sequence: a. renunciation of *jouissance*; b. *plus-de-jouir*; c. object *a*.

The concept of surplus value comes into play when we consider the *historical* manifestation of the renunciation of *jouissance*, a historical moment that coincides with the capitalist mode of production and its social relations, and which Marx saw expressed and concentrated in the commodity form. In Lacan's words: 'To the extent that the market defines as commodity any object of labour whatsoever, this object bears the mark of surplus value [*porte en lui-même quelque chose de la plus-value*]'.[29] In other words, it is of the very essence of commodities under capitalism to express this value, in the same way that it is of the very essence of the object *a* to indicate a loss (of *jouissance*) and generate a surplus. But are the two regimes (libidinal and economical) identical and exchangeable? Are they the two sides of the same coin? If so, should we say that the unconscious is economically overdetermined? Or should we claim that capitalism is the current historical manifestation of the *plus-de-jouir*? That is indeed the question, and one that propels Lacan into new territories, which require a confrontation with historical materialism.[30] It is the same convergence, and the same concern for the 'historical relevance' of psychoanalysis that Lacan has in mind when, a few months later (21 May 1969), he returns to the historical or 'real' manifestation of *jouissance*, and contrasts the ancient world with that of capitalism: whereas a school such as that of the Epicureans had the luxury of a certain distance and innocence in relation to *jouissance*, the subject of capitalism is entirely caught up in it, chained to the logic of the *plus-de-jouir*, and this, as we shall see in greater detail, in such a way that movements of revolt and revolution, such as those that erupted in May 1968, become inevitable, and indeed take on a meaning that did not exist in the ancient world.

Insofar as Marx sees in the commodity form the concealment of the use value and labour power that underpins the exchange value, the only possible enjoyment of the commodity and its process of production is that of a frustration and compensation, which Lacan captures as a *plus-de-jouir*. This means that the supplementary logic or structure of surplus enjoyment is also historically determined. On the one hand, it signals a loss and a frustration: something of the process of production, namely, the surplus value, is always and from the start lost for the working class. On the other hand, the commodity, as an object of consumption, is presented as the only possible satisfaction, which means that satisfaction is, once again, introduced in lieu of *jouissance*, as its substitute or supplement. This means that the commodity, as the expression of the object small *a*, is a *trace* of *jouissance*. To put it slightly differently: what is commonly referred to as the exploitation of the working class is rooted in the expulsion of *jouissance* from labour, that is, and to be more precise, in the confiscation of the surplus value or the operation of abstraction generated by their labour. The economic reality of capitalism is one in which abstract labour is both actualized in, and effaced by, the exchange value; and the surplus value is born of the effacement of the value of labour itself: 'no longer identical to itself, the subject no longer enjoys [*ne jouit plus*]. Something is lost, which is called the *plus-de-jouir*'.[31] Surplus enjoyment is the name of this loss, which is also a gain, or a residue of *jouissance*, incarnated in the commodity form, and especially in its most abstract and universal form, as *money*.

But was the subject ever self-identical? If non-identity and separation – 'alienation' – are the very condition of subjectivity, was labour ever attached to the use value only, and thus free? Lacan's answer is clear, and amounts to a resounding no: non-identity, alienation and loss were never preceded by their opposite; and use value *as such*, that is, as existing independently of exchange value, can only be seen as the economic equivalent of the Thing. Similarly, and as Tomšič puts it, 'because of the asymmetrical relation between abstract and concrete labour, no return to concrete and presumably more authentic forms of labour will abolish the alienation of labour. The alienation of labour is, of course, not a result of capitalism, no more as is discursive alienation. What is its achievement, though, is the objectification of this alienation in a specific commodity', as well as 'the transformation of the subject into labour-power, a commodified, capitalist subject'.[32] Tomšič goes on to claim that commodity fetishism defines an historically specific form of 'constituted' alienation, rooted in 'the misperception of the relation between the appearance of value and the structure that causes this appearance', rather than the 'constitutive' or structural alienation of the subject of desire.[33] In Lacanian terms, and still according to Tomšič, 'this objectification of alienation, its materialisation in a commodity . . . places the subject in the position of the object that satisfies the Other's [namely, the market's] demand for production, the object that is consumed by the Other for the extraction of surplus-object'.[34] And this, he concludes, is precisely Lacan's definition of perversion. As labour-power, the subject is deprived of its subjective position, forced to assume the perverse position of the object of the Other's (or the market's) *jouissance*.

Tomšič's distinction between 'constitutive' and 'constituted' alienation raises the difficult question of the relation between structure and history. As I indicated at the very outset, Lacan does not see an opposition, even less a contradiction between those two levels. Yet he never clarifies their relation. Should we understand the former as designating the transcendental conditions of the latter, or the latter as providing the material conditions of emergence of the former? Is the subject of desire *qua* alienated subject a product of socio-economic relations, or is the empirical subject of capital an instance of a deeper, trans-historical libidinal structure? Does representation precede production, or vice versa? Žižek 'resolves' the issue by adopting a dialectical standpoint, and speaking of the relation between the two levels as one involving the universal and the particular: 'just as Marx simultaneously claimed that all history hitherto is the history of class struggle, *and* that the bourgeoisie is the only true class in the history of humanity, we should say that history is the history of alienation, and that the only true alienation is the capitalist one'.[35] I find this explanation unsatisfactory, and only a semblance of solution, for two reasons. First, the concepts of alienation as used by Marx and Lacan don't refer to the same process. Whilst Marx (in his early work at least) opposes it to the concept of freedom, Lacan doesn't. For Lacan, alienation designates the situation of the subject of desire as such, that is, as separated from itself – a separation that no representation, action or social organization can erase. Lack and loss are forever and irreducibly part of the drama of subjectivity. For Marx, whose concept of alienation (*Entfremdung*) remains indebted to the Hegelian concept of *Entäusserung*, or externalization, of which it signals a bad or failed instance, the horizon of freedom, and a return to self-identity, remains constitutive of the process of self-externalization. Secondly, Žižek is unclear about the meaning of the concept of truth implicit in his reference to 'true class' and 'true alienation'. From the Marxian point of view, or at least that put forward by Žižek, 'true' is synonymous here with 'universal': the only reason why the proletariat is the true class is precisely because it is not recognized as such, because it is an empty class. But this universalist discourse, I would claim, should apply to all groups robbed of their true, actual role, of their voice and identity: whether economic, racial or sexual, one can write a history of the empty class, a history of alienation, without singling one out as *the* universal. Furthermore, to do so – as Marx himself did – is precisely to run the risk of fetishizing a given class or group (the proletariat, the industrial reserve army), and to fall into what Tomšič calls 'scientific' or 'worldview' Marxism – the very Marxism that turned the subject of truth (the proletariat, labour-power) into a subject of knowledge and universal History, the subject who is meant to reach the highest form of self or class-consciousness through the Party, in short, the *normalized* subject.[36] It is to turn the critique of political economy into a master discourse. There can be a *form* of the universal – one, as Rancière claims, that could be defined in terms of the *demos*, that is, the 'surplus community' made up of 'those who have no qualification to rule, which means at once everybody and any one at all'[37] – without any actual instance of that form, any particular group being elevated to the universal as such, and becoming a subject of knowledge or science. I'll return to the possibility of a solution regarding this problem in my conclusion, but will tackle first the manner in which Lacan describes the alienated form of desire under the capitalist mode of production.

Indeed, under capitalism the subject is robbed of its own truth, or the possibility of accessing the libidinal dynamic in which they are caught up. In other words, Lacan seems to acknowledge a specific form of historical alienation, bound up with socio-economic as well as epistemological conditions of existence. In its alienated, 'constituted' form, labour-power is paid according to what the market calls its 'true price', which is itself defined by the exchange value of the commodity. From the point of view of the consistency of the market as expressed in the operation of the capitalist subject, the price is indeed *correct*. Yet, in the product of labour, there is a value that goes unpaid, unrecognized, or covered up by the exchange value: the surplus value or capital that is extracted from labour. This concealed value designates another measure of truth, akin to the unspoken, unseen measure we saw Lacan claim in his critique of the liberal penal system. Tomšič puts it most clearly: 'The problem clearly does not lie in the fact that the value of labour-power would be inadequate or that a more accurate representation of labour-power should be sought, but that labour-power is already produced as structurally inadequate and non-identical.'[38] In other words, the truth of the market and capital cannot be simply denounced as an error (of representation or calculation) that can be rectified by being recognized as such; and the truth of labour is not to be located 'in the presumed adequacy of representation, but in the structural gap that both separates and links it to production'. In short, the truth here is a matter of production – relations of production, labour-power, extraction of value – and not representation. Representation is, if anything, an effect of those relations: a discourse of truth that is mere ideology. Truth in the critical, dialectical sense consists in identifying the terms of a problem, namely, the relations of production that govern discourse, rather than providing the tools and criteria through which a value can be adequately represented and measured. The real problem, and the real *as* problem, is not the value or accurate quantitative representation of labour, but the very existence of labour qua labour-power.

The fact that the surplus value escapes the worker generates a 'frustration' which, in turn, can lead to disputes and even revolutions. But, crucially, and in a way that Marx had anticipated, it can also lead to an ever growing demand to participate in the *jouissance* of the great equivalent or equalizer, namely, money – the supreme commodity in which all commodities are reflected, the universal that is infinitely particularized – and the irresistible force of attraction of consumption, which capital facilitates through credit and low interest rates, thus reinforcing and expanding the transformation of the C-M-C cycle of early capitalism into the M-C-M cycle of late or contemporary capitalism: 'Money is therefore not only *an* object, but *the* object of greed'; and 'not only the object but also the fountainhead of greed'.[39] In that case, the *jouissance* of the worker-consumer is indeed masochistic, a painful excess of pleasure or, as Lacan puts it, 'pleasure-in-pain'. Two realities are therefore at odds: that of labour, and that of capital, and their dispute revolves around truth (more than freedom) in the form of the true price of labour: one, quantitative, ascribes a value to labour; the other, qualitative, inscribes labour as alienation. As a result, the dispute is also between the meaning of the concept of truth in the Marxian critique of political economy, and the meaning and concept of truth in classical political economy. Naturally, the price in question is expressed in monetary terms; and, as Žižek puts it, 'the expression of value in money stems from the fact that an immaterial social relation has to be expressed in a concrete material object'.[40] But the true, qualitative price paid by the worker is of a different kind: it is the price of 'the renunciation of enjoyment [*la renonciation à la jouissance*]', that is, the frustration that is associated with the impossible *jouissance* of the fruit of their labour, as expressed in the surplus value.[41] It is therefore not labour as such that coincides with the renunciation of *jouissance*, but abstract labour as it translates into surplus value and pseudo-*jouissance*. On this particular question then, there seems to be a convergence of views between Marx and Lacan, even if they disagree on the possibility of creating the socio-economic conditions that would eradicate the frustration, or overcome the alienation: capitalism, according to Lacan, introduces the regime of a *plus-de-jouir*, which suspends the *jouissance* of the impossible associated with the relation to the Thing. It replaces the *jouissance* of the impossible with the *plus-de-jouir* of the actual, and productivity.

The articulation of the *objet a* and the *plus-de-jouir* also manifests itself on the side of the relations of consumption, which are dominant in advanced capitalist societies. The function of the *plus-de-jouir* is perhaps most visible in the 'cult' status of the commodity, which presents it as an object of desire in a very specific sense. In the most general sense, and independently of its context, the *objet a* is, first, the cause of desire and, second, essentially and originally lack. It is therefore the mark of the originally split or divided subject. The Thing, as we saw, signals the horizon beyond that split, one we can intimate but never quite reach. Now so long as *jouissance* is associated with the *object a* of a *sexual* drive, it can be satisfied or appeased (5 March 1969), if only partially – either by attaching itself to an organ and the body (through imaginary incorporation or symbolic introjection), or through sublimation (in which case the drive is *zielgehemmt*, deviated from its original sexual goal). All objects of desire, in this sense, fill a gap, or plug the hole of desire as signalling the inaugural division of the subject.[42] All economies are economies of substitution, *bouche-trous* economies: potentially, any empirical, even physiological object (the eye, the mouth, the anus, the voice) is a supplement, a substitute, a plug for a lost object. But what happens with capitalism? It is no longer satisfied, but is caught up in an endless *plus-de-jouir* – an acceleration and intensification of the function of the *objet a*, which goes round and round the chain of desire, like the *furet du bois joli*, whilst being subjected to what Baudrillard, displacing the famous Marxist formulation, called the inevitable 'falling rate of enjoyment'. When *jouissance* is thought as *plus-de-jouir*, and this means as something that satisfies, but never fully, that makes up for the loss of *jouissance*, but never entirely, as something that grants enjoyment whilst perpetuating the *manque-à-jouir*, then the list of objects *a* grows and extends to include objects of culture, industrial production and sublimation. In the age of capitalist (hyper)production and consumption, all objects become objects a, 'vessels of surplus value'.[43] And *jouissance* is itself entirely absorbed in the *plus-de-jouir*. The objects in question all contribute to *jouissance*, yet never amount to *jouissance* as such. They function 'as the place of capture of *jouissance*'.[44] Plentiful and produced at a remarkable rate, they provoke and titillate our desire, yet only emphasize our *manque-à-jouir*. They allow, indeed force us to enjoy, but partially, by bits. They provide, Lacan says, 'nibbles [*lichettes*] of *jouissance*'.[45] Our world fills with substitutes of *jouissance*, which are bits of nothing, crumbs of *jouissance*. In truth, the only available *jouissance* is the *jouissance* of one's own constituted alienation: it is the perverse enjoyment of one's servitude. In his long radio interview in 1970, Lacan speaks of 'the necessity of the *plus-de-jouir* in order for the [capitalist] machine to function'; and of the 'hole' – the hole of *jouissance* – that this mechanism plugs.[46] In other words, capitalism produces an endless lack, a series of bottomless pits, which the *plus-de-jouir*, as bound up with surplus-value, fills frantically but only momentarily:

> On the one hand, surplus-value is accumulated in order to increase the means of production of capital. On the other hand, it extends consumption, without which the production in question would be in vain. In any event, it is incapable of generating a *jouissance* that would signal a slowdown of this model of production.[47]

On the contrary: it demands that the subject enjoys this lack, identifies with it, and assumes the position of commodity. It aggravates the subject's lack or loss of being through the production of a surplus-object, an accumulation without end. As the dominant 'cause of desire', surplus value is responsible for 'the extensive and thus insatiable production of the *manque-à-jouir*'.[48] It converts the subject's lack-in-being into a commodity surplus. As Žižek puts it, under capitalism the superego is revealed in the injunction to enjoy the 'sign' or 'cult' value of the commodity. It 'does not enjoin us to follow our duty against the temptation of succumbing to the pleasure provided by the use value of a commodity ("Do not buy stoned-washed jeans – even if they are comfortable to wear, you are thereby endorsing imperialist ideology!"); on the contrary, the commodity's sign value, the ideology associated with it, enjoins us to enjoy its use value even if we really do not feel any need for it.'[49]

Capitalism thus renders enjoyment impossible, even lost. That is what it desires. An object of consumption will never measure up to the lost object (object *a*); and accumulation will never compensate for the feeling of loss and frustration associated with the renunciation of *jouissance*. All there is is lack, elevated to the nth power: a *plus-de-jouir* in the sense of a no-more-enjoyment that is also and at the same time a *plus-de-jouir* in the sense of an excess, or an ever more. Within the capitalist economy, there are just too many holes. It keeps producing them, and they siphon off desire. Behind every hole one plugs, there is a bigger one: one's entire vital energy is sucked into this punctured reality. I myself become full of holes, fragmented, dispersed. Such is the madness of capitalism, one that has generated its own rationality. Capitalism is paradoxical in that it is a formidable apparatus of production, but one that produces lack: it produces *through* lack and *for* it. Without it, it ceases to exist. Its problem is to know how to create more lack, how to turn lack into the condition and substance of all relations. This is the paradox of a system that manages to use resources, an entire ecosystem, life itself to the bone, yet through overproduction. The *plus-de-jouir* is the tragic condition of the subject of capitalism: I can't go on, yet I must go on.

May 1968 was a formidable and ambiguous reaction to that frustration, and a cry for the right to *jouissance*, over and beyond the *plus-de-jouir*, which is always a *manque-à-jouir*. It was a rejection of that other discourse, the 'university discourse', for which knowledge is the master signifier, and which, like the master's discourse, is a discourse of authority. The knowledge that Lacan targets here is the kind that has close ties with power – with capitalist power especially – and has taken root in universities, thus subordinating the *question* of knowledge to the imperatives of surplus value: the current epoch signals the 'absolutisation of the market of knowledge', and the reduction of knowledge to the commodity form.[50] The 'credit-point', known in France as the *unité de valeur*, or unit of value, 'the little piece of paper that they want to issue you with … is the sign of what knowledge will progressively become in this market that one calls the University'.[51] Knowledge is thus increasingly detached from true science. As Bruce Fink rightly points out, in his later work Lacan dissociates true scientific work, in which he includes his own ('the analyst's discourse'), from the university discourse. Whereas the former 'tries to come to grips with the real, to maintain the difficulties posed by apparent logical and/or physical contradictions', the latter amounts to a mere totalizing, encyclopaedic endeavour 'in the service of the master signifier', which produces *and* excludes the subject of the unconscious.[52] There is therefore a parallel between the subjectivity of the worker and that of the student and researcher:

> In this situation, there is therefore also something that, whilst paid according to the true price of knowledge [*son vrai prix de savoir*] as defined by the norms of the market of science, is nonetheless obtained for nothing [*pour rien*]. This is what I have called the *plus-de-jouir*.

Within the socio-economics of capitalism, which includes relations of material production as well as knowledge, a certain amount of work goes unrecognized, concealed: a quantity of work, and thus a value, is obtained 'for nothing', for a pittance. A surplus is extracted from the subject, despite themselves, and against the background of a barrier to their *jouissance*. A 'false' form of *jouissance* is extracted, one that corresponds to the extraction of surplus value. So, on the one hand we have this surplus (of value and enjoyment), and on the other this 'nothing' or 'pittance'.

Jouissance of the capitalist subject aside (but, since Lacan's time, every subject has become a capitalist, that is, a *homo economicus* defined by their human capital), then, capitalism amounts to the organization of collective frustration: as a *plus-de-jouir* that is the 'perversion' of *jouissance*. The discontent of civilization is expressed in the form of 'a *plus-de-jouir* [a negation *and* a surplus of enjoyment] obtained from the renunciation of *jouissance*'.[53] The 'symptom', Lacan goes on to explain, is 'the way in which everyone suffers in their relation to *jouissance*, to the extent that they partake in it only through the function of the *plus-de-jouir*'.[54] And that of which one is frustrated, which is unpaid, is *truth*. To be more precise: the only truth that is recognized is an abstract one (the truth of abstract labour). Such is the reason why Lacan says that what was really on strike in May 1968 was truth itself: students and workers demanded the recognition of the true price or value, and of the stupidity (Lacan even says '*connerie*') of a form of labour captured in relations of surplus value. They demanded the recognition of their own *malaise* or discontent as a *jouissance* perverted as *plus-de-jouir*. They demanded the recognition of a form of knowledge other than that of the market, of a truth other than that of the form of commodity, and of themselves as subjects of another truth and another knowledge, disentangled from relations of domination. At the same time, and more naïvely, they demanded a return to an impossible *jouissance*, a return to the Thing. As such, May 1968 was both a rejection of the university and capitalist discourses *and* a nostalgic appeal to *jouissance*, to the possibility of a unified subject, a Law (and thus Master). It was at once rebellious *and* nostalgic, if not reactionary.

With his analysis of the *plus-de-jouir*, Lacan seems to have crossed into a different kind of analytic – a critique of the present and of the deep connection, indeed the intertwining between political and libidinal economy. In that period, Lacan seems to recognize something like a history or historicity of desire, and one that would possibly require that psychoanalysis itself *begin* as historical critique: the structure of desire is available only in its historical form, which itself modifies its structure. But I would claim that Lacan had begun to recognize such an intertwining, and the need for an historical-critical account of desire, earlier on. You will recall how, in the piece that he wrote with Cénac, which is echoed in a number of subsequent writings, including in Seminars VII and XX, Lacan reflects on his age as one of 'crisis', one, he believes, that can be attributed to the rise of the liberal paradigm, based on the concepts of utility and interest, and the advent of what he calls 'the man of pleasure'.[55] Why, I asked, speak of 'crisis'? Because the 'naturalist emancipation', most manifest in today's market principles and compulsive consumerism – has failed. And his assessment of liberal criminology and penology was meant to reveal such a dead end. In his later work, Lacan returns to this crisis or failure, but this time from the standpoint of the *plus-de-jouir* and the *objet a* – still, for him, indicative of an order beyond 'utility', one that he sees as *real*, if not material: the socio-economic substructure of discourse, he claims, are 'the most real' and 'the real itself'.[56] As a result, his appreciation of the function of the law changes: he now envisages it from the point of view not of crime and punishment, of the struggle between the imaginary and the symbolic, of the Thing and the Law, but of the object small *a* and *jouissance*. At the same time, his assessment of May 1968, of the student 'contestation' and the paralyzing strikes, confirms his diagnosis of crisis – one that he sees as internal to a new form of power, namely, 'liberal' or 'capitalist' power.[57] The concept of the *plus-de-jouir*, and its connection with the concept of the *objet a*, are intimately bound up with an analysis of the *malaise* or discontent of the age of capitalism. That concept is made possible, if not necessary, by an historical 'turning point' (*tournant*), through which Lacan realizes that desire is always caught up in, and possibly the expression of, a field of power and knowledge, in relation to which the discourse of psychoanalysis is to situate itself, and resist by imagining other regimes of desire, which include a different relation to oneself as a subject of truth, and a different concept of truth. Does this mean that psychoanalytic concepts are themselves effects of historical situations, or that historical events can trigger the need for new analytic concepts? Does the discourse of desire need to move away from a metapsychology, or does it need to enact a constant to and fro between metapsychology and historical critique?

We saw how Lacan engages in such a critique through Marx. However, the historical-critical approach I have privileged is genealogical, in the sense developed by Foucault. It is one in which the conditions of subjectivation (which would include, but not be reducible to, economic exploitation) and discourses (which include political economy and psychopathology) aren't exclusively socio-economic. In fact, Foucault goes as far as to identify the conditions of emergence of the schema of desire in late Antiquity, thereby suggesting that the subject of desire is itself a historical construction, and the effect of a transformation – indeed an internalization – of the connection between truth and subjectivity, one that was subsequently developed and systematized through techniques of the self, such as confession and spiritual direction, and inscribed within a new conception of the body as flesh. I have reason to doubt Foucault's claim, as I see evidence of the analytic of desire already in the Platonic and Aristotelian corpus. But I do maintain that there is something that is historically distinctive about the *modern* subject of desire, and that Lacan – at times, explicitly, at times only implicitly – situates his own discourse in relation, and at times in opposition, to modernity. That period is characterized by the emergence of a range of discourses – biology, psychiatry, the science of sexuality, political economy, law – which share a normative and normalizing framework, one that operates alongside and through a range of institutions (the family, the market, the law, the state, the hospital, the university, etc.). In other words, I see the value of Lacan's work in his libidinal constructivism, which borrows elements from psychoanalysis, the social sciences, philosophy and mathematics in order to imagine a different subject of desire, one that would escape the grip of such normative and normalizing practices. At times, the subject in question seems to extend and generalize a specific moment of the phenomenological position of consciousness according to Hegel. At other times, the subject of desire is defined in relation to the moral law, and modelled after the Kantian ideal of pure autonomy. Finally, and perhaps most adequately, his resistance to the modern framing of the subject of desire takes the form of a Marxism stripped of its positivism and dogmatism, and focuses on that subject as an empty or abstract universal, or as the subject of capitalism. The traditional concepts of truth and freedom aren't dismissed in the process. Rather, they become the object of a new thinking, aimed at the possibility of a new relation between subjects, and of the subject's relation to themselves.

At that point, the question of the relation between structure and history becomes less important: for if every structure is itself a construction, the true question becomes that of knowing the sort of subjects that we are, the role that desire plays in that process, and what mechanisms, if any, could be used to construct ourselves as subjects of desire differently. The question is no longer one of essence, one of knowing what desire *is*. Rather, it is a critical or modal question: how do we desire, how does desire operate, what is your desire? Whether as structure (in the topological sense) or history, the conditions of experience of oneself as a subject of desire can't amount to a complete and definitive analytic, nor be rooted in something such as a purely transcendental form of subjectivity (albeit reconfigured as unconscious). And the schema that is at stake here is one that is concerned not with what it makes possible (with the conditions of possible experience), but with what it produces; not with its signification, but with the manner in which it operates or works. Desire, in that respect, is an assemblage or dispositive that produces effects, shapes lives. It designates corporeal states and relations, rather than representations. It is embodied in relations of power and discourse, but also signals alternatives, openings, lines of flight. In that respect, Lacan's position is closer than we might think to that of Deleuze, who writes: 'Desire is never a natural or spontaneous determination', but an 'assemblage'.[58] Feudalism, for example, is an assemblage that inaugurates new relations with animals (with the horse, for example), with the land (with the holy land, for example), with women (with the Dame of courtly love, about whom Lacan himself had much to say). Those assemblages, Deleuze insists, contain relations of power, but aren't reducible to them: even Foucault's analytic of power isn't able to account for the micro-physics of forces and affections that define desire. For ultimately, they indicate a degree or quantity of *potentia*, rather than relations of *potestas* or *imperium*. As such, they can signal a form of voluptuousness that exceeds the many forms of *jouissance* described by Lacan, as well as the regime of *aphrodisia* problematized by Foucault, or indeed any regime of pleasure – a voluptuousness associated with the increase of one's power to act, feel and think.

6

Conclusion

Wege, nicht Werke. 'Paths, not works.' This motto, under which Heidegger placed his *Gesamtausgabe*, applies equally to Lacan, who published only a few works in his lifetime, and whose thought took the form of a teaching and often improvised performance. His *parole* opens up lines of investigation and paths of various kinds, which often turn back on themselves, before starting afresh. But they don't converge towards a single point or main thesis, or amount to anything like a system. We could also say that Lacan appropriated for psychoanalysis Canguilhem's famous definition of philosophy, according to which it is 'a reflection for which all foreign material [*toute matière étrangère*] is good and, we would gladly say, for which all good material must be foreign [*étrangère*]'.[1] To be sure, Lacan only ever considered one object, namely, the subject of desire, or the unconscious; and throughout, we saw him hold on to, and problematize, a certain idea of truth, to which the discourse of the analyst is bound. But the subject of desire and the truth for which it stands take on many forms; and their structure turned out to be infinitely plastic, as Lacan's late topological schematization revealed. As such, the subject in question can be approached from many angles and perspectives. Lacan did not hesitate to draw inspiration from philosophy, literature, anthropology, law, political economy and mathematics, at the risk of seeming inconsistent, if not incoherent. We saw him read Freud with Hegel, against a naturalistic, positivist conception of psychiatry and metapsychology. But we also saw him supplement Freud (and Hegel) with structuralism, and the latter with certain developments in topology. We saw him read Kant (with Sade) against Spinoza and Hegel, and then Marx against Kant. And we saw him mobilize all those resources against utilitarianism. If there is one lesson to learn from Lacan, it is that of a subject whose desire is not motivated by pleasure, and whose agency cannot be accounted for by the central concepts of the liberal, bourgeois order – concepts of utility, motive, calculation, interest, etc. *Jouissance*, he insists throughout, has nothing to do with satisfaction or appeasement.

To move closer to the specific framework within which I approached his texts and seminars, I would say that their value consists in the depth of their engagement with what I take to be major presuppositions of the western morphology of desire and of its modern regime in particular, by which I mean not only the analytic of sexuality, but the dialectic and politics of recognition, as well as the liberal and utilitarian rationality of self-interest, which also underpins bourgeois criminology and penology. In each case, Lacan was able to shift some of the most deeply entrenched lines of thought, to loosen the grip of those rationalities on the subject of desire and question their basic presuppositions. We saw him engage with, and resist, the clinical norms he inherited from the psychopathology of the nineteenth and early-twentieth century, and which associate desire with sexuality, define the latter according to strict coordinates and a natural norm, deviations from which led to diagnoses of abnormality and pathology, and the invention of a range of therapeutic, orthopaedic measures meant to normalize the desiring, sexualized subject. We saw him drive a wedge between desire, as defining the depths and opacity of consciousness, and a natural instinct or force, fully visible and accessible to the medical gaze. In place of this natural sexual instinct, we saw him frame desire in terms of a different gaze, the gaze of the imaginary and a dialectic of recognition, which produces its own (narcissistic) tendencies. Yet, increasingly aware of the limits of the paradigm of recognition, from a theoretical as well as clinical point of view, Lacan moved away from that central concept of modern social and political thought. Instead, he turned to another, symbolic paradigm, that of the Father and the Law, in which the drama or dialectic of desire, qua desire of recognition, was to find its moment of resolution. In doing so, however, he returned the subject of desire to its pre-modern, possibly archaic correlate, in what can be seen as a regressive move. For what, I asked, is the value of a system that detaches desire from its naturalistic and clinical normativity, but only to reinsert it within the paradigm of a moral, transcendent law, and the phallocratic authority of the Father? What is the purpose of exchanging a naturalistic, orthopaedic system of norms with a moral and symbolic one, which affects only the *form* of our desire? These questions came to a head in Chapters 3 and 4, which revealed the value (anticipated, no doubt, by Klein's work on criminality) of Lacan's critique of liberal criminology and penology, focusing on the rationality of interest and motive, and drawing our attention to the fragility of its naturalistic underpinnings. These chapters also revealed the limits of that critique, given the purely prohibitive (and thus also transgressive) role he attributes to the legal order – a role he tried to rectify and overcome in his reading of Kant as a critic of utilitarian morality and politics. So, on the one hand, the symbolic moment of the Law, which comes from without and above, is supposed to suspend the (nostalgic) desire for total unity (with the Mother) and the *jouissance* of her possession. Yet the Law itself remains suspended between the *jouissance* of its own transgression and a desire for punishment born of the deeper desire to transgress the primal prohibition. In *The Ethics of Psychoanalysis* and other related texts, Lacan was drawn to Kant's formalistic approach to the moral law, in which he found the purest expression of desire as determined internally and a priori by the categorical imperative, and leading to a new form of *jouissance*, that of the Impossible, or *das Ding*.

Had Lacan's thought culminated in that Kantian moment, or had our reading stopped at that point, we would have been forgiven for seeing the trajectory of that thought as an interesting but ultimately unsuccessful attempt to wrest the subject of desire from its naturalization through the *psychopathia sexualis* and even psychoanalysis of the sexual instinct, the philosophical anthropology of interest, motive and the maximization of utility, or the psychology and sociology of recognition. But our exploration of Lacan's texts from the late 1960s and early 1970s revealed a different, potentially more fruitful line of thought, in that it indicated the possibility of a way out of the liberal construction of the subject of desire altogether. I say potentially, because much of what we focused on remained undeveloped and exploratory. Only in his late work, when he reworks some of the key terms that are not norms – *jouissance* as *plus-de-jouir*, objects small *a*, and most of all the real – does he really twist free of the modern analytic of desire and begin to open another space for thinking the subject of desire, outside, or at least fully aware of, the dangers of the master discourse, of the discourse of truth and the relations of power inherent in the discourse of science. Only then does he begin to think of desire as a real, historical process, as essentially productive rather than representative. By then, the analytic discourse has become compatible with critique – as genealogy and as a critique of the present, which also means as critique of the economic, capitalist framing of desire, which can then also be read back into some of his earlier analyses, such as his text on psychoanalysis and criminology. This advance, and the transformation or creation of concepts with which it coincided, can be attributed to the role of the Real in that period.

In my Introduction I spoke of the Real, by which I think Lacan ultimately intended the subject of desire as such, or the unconscious as the very 'object' of psychoanalytic discourse. Yet this object is like no other, in that it is nowhere to be found as such, in the flesh, but only in the effects it produces, negatively as it were. It can never be stared in the face, made to speak in and from itself, as phenomenologists would say. It can only be approached through its many signifiers (the Other, the phallus, the Thing, the object small a, etc.). The Real unfolds *at the limit* – at the limit of the Imaginary and the Symbolic, of language and consciousness: '*Le Réel n'a d'existence, qu'à rencontrer du Symbolique et de l'Imaginaire, l'arrêt*'.[2] It begins where the Symbolic and the Imaginary end, except that we can't follow it there, for words fail us, and language can only symbolize. The Real signals the 'presence' of a crack, a gaping hole (*trou*) at the heart of subjectivity, but one we can't go down. The unconscious is 'the Real ... the Real insofar as it is *troué*.[3] Equally, though, the Real is the hole that punctures reality, this massive hole at the heart of the reality we perceive, imagine, represent, speak, etc. It speaks ('*Ça parle*') but in the only manner that it can, namely, indirectly and negatively, only as the Impossible – whether in the form of the object *a*, which doesn't penetrate the field of the specular image, that of non-phallic *jouissance* (of the Thing, the Mother, or the Law – all of which are figures of the Impossible), which escapes the play of signifiers and language, or that of the nothing (*le rien*), which the anorexic desires.[4] The Real penetrates, conquers and colonizes reality, but its empirical objects are only ever substitutes, fillers (*bouche-trous*). For the real object *a* – say, the breast for the oral drive – is essentially lost, and never rediscovered or regained as such. And the drive, whether oral or anal, phallic or scopic, is itself only ever partial, only the fragment of a reality that will never be pieced back together. The real, lost object is constituted as a remainder or residue of the imaginary and the symbolic: it figures neither in the specular image nor in the Ego-ideal, both of which it nonetheless props up, from without as it were. But this exteriority doesn't exclude it from the structure, as Lacan increasingly realized. The real is itself structural, and structures as a hole. Hence Lacan's topological schematization of desire, his late onto-nodology.

But, in recognizing desire as a hole and speaking of an irreducibly split or cracked subject, one marked by difference or non-identity, do we necessarily need to understand it as a lack? Is lack the defining feature of subjectivity? Or can we define the Real itself as the split or crack of reality itself, but one that signals the excess that draws the subject in, the abundance of desire itself? Can we define desire as the crack through which the depths of the Real erupt, and are experienced, rather than as the manifestation of a forever incomplete and deficient subjectivity? Could the negativity of desire be overturned, not as a (false and misleading) moment of reconciliation with the lost object, or even as the promise or hope of that reunion, but as the uneasiness and disquiet that propel us anew and afresh into the world, beyond our own neuroses and perversions? Could desire become the name for the subject's self-overcoming?

Not every *trou*, after all, need be a '*troumatisme*'. The good thing about holes is that they need not turn into melancholy and a longing to return to the lost object, or even its partial substitute and fixations. They also, and perhaps above all, make 'invention' and 'construction' possible.[5] To be sure, this construction, as Lacan clearly recognized, can be economic, and amount to the atomization of the Big Hole into an endless production of small holes. It can take the form of the systematic organization of social relations as relations of lack, or, which amounts to the same thing, of relations between subjects as relations between commodities. As we saw, the object *a* as surplus enjoyment and 'spoliation of jouissance' can't be identified with the breast that the subject internalized or the excrement with which it identified in its childhood, in other words with a partial, supplementary object of a sexual drive. It is identified with a mere object of envy, and an object of *jouissance* related to the other's desire of that object. As such, it is a reconfiguration of a system of relations organized around lack. But is that Lacan's most important point, and the lesson we need to draw? Or is the point, instead, to recognize specific historical constructions of desire, which favour lack, loss, nostalgia, envy and an object-driven form of *jouissance*, on the one hand, and another possible assemblage of desire, oriented towards a form of excess and plenitude, one that is at the same time irreducible to sublimation, which is itself another filler or second best?

Constructive assemblages, from love and friendship to art, philosophy and political communities, signal the existence of alternative forms of desire. Of course, Orpheus can be seen as the tale of the Impossible, that is, of the impossible reunion with the lost object and the cause of desire, of the impossibility of looking the object of desire in the eye and seeing it for what it is, of the impossibility of coming face to face with the Real. But, with Blanchot, it can also be read as the descent into the opacity of consciousness and reason, into the night that is not the negation of day and light, but their origin and depth, and the fabric or stuff of art: the night of the Real, in which not all cows are black. This is the desire of the work, or the desire that the work brings to light, and in the process of which it deconstructs or undoes itself as an *object* (or even a Thing) in order to become a *work*. It is into this night, where everything disappears, that Orpheus plunges, but it is precisely by plunging into it that he splits open the darkness: art, 'The Gaze of Orpheus' tells us, is 'the power by which night discloses itself'.

To write, Deleuze claims in a text largely inspired by Blanchot, doesn't consist in 'imposing a form on a lived content (*une matière vécue*)', and the act of writing 'exceeds all liveable or lived content'.[6] Not, mind you, in favour of a death inherent to life itself, and to what would resemble a death drive, but of a dying that signals a threshold, a passage to the limit and the beginning of another life. In the words of Blanchot:

> Desire, writing, do not remain in place, but pass one over the other: these are not play on words, for desire is always desire of dying, not

> a wish. And yet, desire is related to *Wunsch*, and is a nondesire too – the powerless power that traverses writing – just as writing is the desired, undesired torment which endures everything, even impatience. Dying desire, desire to die, we live these together – not that they coincide – in the obscurity of the interim.[7]

In this dying, which is without end and which my own death can't suspend or interrupt, since it suspends *my* life as being-towards-death, along with its anxiety, its projects and its 'unsurpassable horizon', desire turns me away from myself, from my star and the entire cosmic order. The desire in question doesn't unfold under a starry sky and doesn't bathe in the light of the firmament and consideration. Rather, and in Blanchot's words, it sinks deep into the Night, which is not the flip side or negation of day, but the life of the 'neuter', or of 'disaster'. Beyond any 'curiosity' and 'knowledge', but also beyond the unconscious search for the lost object, it unfolds as the desire of writing. If, in the end, desire is indeed 'this detour through which 'I' am disconsidered'[8] or 'I' find myself turned away from my original 'consideration', it takes place in and as *writing*. Minimally, writing is the experience of the dispossession of the self, in which its narcissistic desire, or the care of itself, is led astray and adrift, carried away towards the impersonal life of the neuter. If, as Heidegger believed, death is what individualizes me absolutely, and that through which this life indeed becomes *my* life, then the turning of desire, as the desire of writing, consists in the impossibility of my *own* death, and of myself as ownness. It consists rather of an infinitive and impersonal 'dying', that is, of an event that is without beginning or end, anarchic and interminable, and coincides with what Lacan calls the Real. 'I' must die so that 'dying' may take place, and the Real may speak. From that point of view, the desire of writing isn't a wish or drive emanating from the self, but a power without power – without, that is, the power of existence. It's a desire that signals the limit of existence and reality, and of death as the limit and condition of all possibilities, including those of the Imaginary and the Symbolic. Death, insofar as it is *mine*, is indeed still indicative of my power. But the desire of writing signals another form of life, a pure event that is unlike anything I may have lived. This is the extent to which 'dying' would not be the negation or impossibility of life, but its highest realization, and the ultimate and most joyful expression of desire: 'I' would never be more alive than dying, of a life that would precisely not be that of my own, lived experience, or of consciousness, but of this burgeoning and flourishing unconscious that the self suffocates, or at least *reduces*. At stake, here, is an unlived *matter*, far more decisive that anything lived: an event in which 'I' am finally able to die, and in the vanishing of which something far greater and more beautiful than my own memories, my past, in short, my *Erlebnis*, is able to emerge; a life that is no longer *my* life, nor even *life*, but *a* life, which is neither particular nor universal, but impersonal. When 'I' am no longer there, when there is no longer anyone, there remains the impersonal, in which writing takes place. To be sure, the 's/he' of writing is still a person, even though it is the most impersonal. It's the person that literature can't do without, but it's a person that withdraws and vanishes in the face of the pure event. It's when the writer crosses that threshold, and when desire, lost in the depths of Night, and far from the torments of existence, has become the writing of disaster, that life reaches its highest expression. No doubt, the writer suffers from feeling things and creatures to that extent. But that suffering is also their joy – the unparalleled joy of inexhaustible and infinite Being, the joy of knowing that they are condemned to err and never know, but in an erring that is deeper than any exploration of the world.

Infinitely *désœuvré*, the writer can now abandon themself to this desire that is not *with a view* to enjoyment, but that *is* enjoyment – '*désir demeuré désir*'.[9] At that point, *jouissance* itself has slipped away to give way to a life of pure intensity and the *voluptuousness* of the Real. This is the point at which life itself becomes something altogether different, something that unfolds at the limit of life itself (in the form of the Imaginary and the Symbolic), in close proximity with the unlivable: an *expérience intérieure*. In one of his most striking statements, Foucault describes experience as the attempt 'to reach that point of life that is closest to what can't be lived [*l'invivable*]' and for which 'the greatest intensity is required'.[10] The aim of experience, he goes on to say, is

> . . . to tear [*arracher*] the subject from itself, to act in such a way that it is no longer recognizable, no longer itself; to bring it to its own annihilation, or dissolution. It is an enterprise of desubjectivation. It is the idea of this liminal experience, in which the subject is torn from itself, which was significant for me when reading Nietzsche, Bataille, and Blanchot.[11]

What if, in the end, the highest expression of desire was *liminal*, or the experience of life (of intensity) at the limit of the Real? What if, rather than self-identifying, it consisted in tearing oneself away from oneself, and becoming Other, through writing, yes, but also through other 'constructions' and 'inventions', whether erotic or political?

NOTES

Introduction

1. J. Lacan, S XX.
2. J. Lacan, S XXIII.
3. See J. Lacan, S XXII, seminars of 8 April and 15 April 1975. A full transcript of the seminars, which the Seuil is yet to publish, is available here: http://www.valas.fr/IMG/pdf/s22_r.s.i.pdf. A printed version of the seminars was published in *Ornicar?*, 2–5, 1975.
4. In that respect, this book can be read as a response and alternative to Joan Copjec's *Read My Desire: Lacan Against the Historicists* (Cambridge, MA: MIT Press, 1994), which accuses Foucault of 'historicism', by which the author means his inability to recognize 'a principle or a subject that "transcends" the regime of power he analyzes' (6) in order to properly analyze the regime in question. By privileging history over structure, and the model of conflict and war over that of language and signs, genealogy would fail to carry out its critical aim and inevitably lead to a new form of idealism. This book aims to build a case for a genealogical approach to Lacan, and indeed explore the ways in which Lacan himself can be seen to contribute to such an approach. As such, it rejects the alternative Copjec presents us with: either, following Lacan, to recognize desire as structure, or, following Foucault, to 'want to have nothing to do with desire' (14).
5. Miguel de Beistegui, *The Government of Desire: A Genealogy of the Liberal Subject* (Chicago: Chicago University Press, 2018).
6. M. Foucault, *Les aveux de la chair* (Paris: Gallimard, 2018), 354–5; *Dire vrai sur soi-même: Conférences prononcées à l'Université Victoria de Toronto*, 1982, edited by Henri-Paul Fruchaud and Daniele Lorenzini (Vrin: Paris, 2017), 283. See also Daniele Lorenzini, 'The Emergence of Desire: Notes Toward a Political History of the Will', *Critical Inquiry* 45 (Winter 2019), 466–7.
7. M. Foucault, *The History of Sexuality, Volume 1: An Introduction*, translated by Robert Hurley (New York: Random House, 1978), 81.

8. M. Foucault, *The History of Sexuality, Volume 1*, op. cit., 83. See also J. Lacan, E 125–49/102–22.

9. M. Foucault, *The History of Sexuality, Volume 1*, op. cit. 89–90. Translation modified.

10. Ibid., 90.

11. Ibid.

12. Adam Smith, *The Theory of Moral Sentiments*, edited by Knud Hakkonssen (Cambridge: Cambridge University Press), I.iii.2.

13. M. Foucault, 'What is Critique?' translated by Lisa Hochroth and Catherine Porter, in Sylvère Lotringer (ed.), *The Politics of Truth* (Los Angeles: Semiotext(e), 1997), 47.

14. J. Lacan, S XVI 289; S XX 75/80–1; S XXIII 51/38–9.

15. J. Lacan, XI 250/224–5.

16. J. Lacan, S XI 293/263. These questions form the basis of Chapter 3.

17. J. Lacan, S XI 295, 293/265, 263.

18. J. Lacan, S XI 256, 294/230, 264.

19. J. Lacan, S VIII 42–4/30–2.

20. The ethics in question is elevated to a basic principle in the rules and guiding principles of the *École française de psychanalyse*, which Lacan founded on 21 June 1964. In his opening statement, he writes: 'Ethics of psychoanalysis, which is the praxis of its theory' (AE 232).

21. J. Lacan, S VII 208/177.

22. See A. Badiou, *Théorie du sujet* (Paris: Le Seuil, 1982); *Le Séminaire. Vérité et sujet, 1987–1988* (Paris: Fayard, 2017); *L'être et l'événement* (Paris: Le Seuil, 1988), Meditation 37 (Descartes/Lacan); *Conditions* (Paris: Le Seuil, 1992), 277–326; *Le Séminaire. Lacan. L'antiphilosophie 3, 1994–1995* (Paris: Fayard, 2013); *Logique des mondes* (Paris: Seuil, 2006), Book VII; *Il n'y a pas de rapport sexuel. Deux leçons sur 'L'Étourdit de Lacan*, with B. Cassin (Paris: Fayard, 2010); *Jacques Lacan, passé, present : dialogue avec Élisabeth Roudinesco* (Paris: Le Seuil, 2012).

23. Alain Badiou, *Vérité et sujet*, op. cit., 9; also 183–4. Elsewhere, however, Badiou equates the subject of science, the Cartesian subject (of 'mathematical truths'), and the subject of psychoanalysis (as expressed in the matheme), and claims that Lacan remained committed to the rationalist project of the Enlightenment throughout his life. See *Vérité et sujet*, op. cit., 75; *Lacan.*

L'antiphilosophie 3, op. cit., 124–6; Radio Interview with Christine Goémé, France Culture, 5 May 2001 (https://podcloud.fr/podcast/les-nuits-de-france-culture/episode/alain-badiou-je-considere-que-lacan-est-un-homme-des-lumieres-cest-un-rationaliste-integral). I will return to the subject of truth in psychoanalysis, and Badiou's interpretation of it, in Chapter 3.

24. This is something Badiou himself recognizes: in the end, Lacan's mathemes are only 'quasi-mathemes', for they are not *of* being as such (*Vérité et sujet*, op. cit., 98).

25. A. Badiou, *Conditions*, op. cit., 254–6; A. Badiou, *Lacan. L'antiphilosophie 3*, op. cit., 158–9.

Chapter One

1. J. Lacan, E, 247/205.

2. See S. Freud, *The Interpretation of Dreams* (SE V 533–49). See also Erik Porath, 'Vom Reflexbogen zum psyschichen Apparat: Neurologie und Psychoanalyse um 1900', *Berichte zur Wissenschaftsgeschichte* (Wiesbaden: Akademische Verlagsgesellschaft Athenaion), March 2009, 32 (1): 53–69.

3. This is actually what Samo Tomšič argues in *The Capitalist Unconscious* (London: Verso, 2015), 120. I'll return to the question of pleasure, and its difference from what Lacan calls *jouissance*, throughout the book, but especially in Chapter 5.

4. J. Lacan, S, III 16/7–8.

5. J. Lacan, S XI, 197/176; E, 147–8/121; E, 518/431; E, 266–89/220–39.

6. See also Malcolm Bowie, *Lacan* (London: Fontana Press, 1991: *Marx and Lacan*),131–4; M. Borch-Jacobsen, *Lacan: The Absolute Master*, trans. Douglas Brick (Stanford: Stanford University Press, 1991), 205–21; Rudolf Bernet, *Force – Pulsion – Désir. Une autre philosophie de la psychanalyse* (Paris: Vrin, 2103), 196, 230.

7. J. Lacan, E, 690/579.

8. On Lacan's return to Freud, see Jean-Michel Rabaté, 'Lacan's Turn to Freud', in J. M. Rabaté (ed.), *The Cambridge Companion to Lacan* (Cambridge: Cambridge University Press, 2003), 1–24.

9. J. Lacan, E, 178–88/145–53; E 151–92/75–81.

10. See Henri Wallon, 'Comment se développe chez l'enfant la notion de corps propre', *Journal de psychologie*, November–December 1931, 705–48. Wallon was the first to use the expression '*stade du miroir*' – a fact that Lacan was not keen to emphasize (or keen not to emphasize). For further details on Lacan's careful omission of his debt, see E. Roudinesco, 'The Mirror Stage, an obliterated archive', trans. Barbara Bray, in J. M. Rabaté (ed.), *The Cambridge Companion to Lacan*, op. cit., 27; Mikkel Borch-Jacobsen, *Lacan: The Absolute Master*, op. cit.,. 46–7 and 248–9. See also Charlotte Bühler, *Soziologische und psychologische Studien über das erste Lebensjahr* (Iena: Fischer, 1927).

11. L. Harrison Matthews, 'Visual stimulation and ovulation in pigeons', *Proceedings of the Royal Society*, Series B (Biological Sciences), number 845, 3 February 1939, Vol. 126: 557–60.

12. See Wolfgang Köhler, *Intelligenzprüfungen an Menschenaffen* (Berlin: Springer, 1921); Rémy Chauvin, 'Contribution à l'étude physiologique du criquet pèlerin et du déterminisme des phénomènes grégaires', *Annales de la société entomologique de France*, 1941, 3ème trimeste, Vol. 110.

13. J. Lacan, E 170/139.

14. J. Lacan, S II 241/239.

15. J. Lacan, S I 122/122. See also: J. Lacan, S I 138/138.

16. Lacan first refers to the Dutch anatomist Louis Bolk (1866–1930) in 'Les complexes familiaux dans la formation de l'individu. Essai d'analyse d'une fonction en psychologie' (1938), *Autres écrits*, 34–5. Many references to his work will follow. See for example J. Lacan, 'Presentation on Psychical Causality' (186/152). On the reception of Bolk's work in France in the late 1920s, and in psychoanalytic circles in particular, see Marc Levivier, 'La fœtalisation de Louis Bolk', *Essaim* 1/2011 (no 26), 153–68. Bolk's most important, yet still programmatic, work is *Das Problem der Menschenwerdung*, G. Fischer, 1926.

17. J. Lacan, E 96, 186/78, 152.

18. J. Lacan E 97/78.

19. Kojève himself was interested in the connection between Hegel and Freud. He had planned to collaborate with Lacan on a piece for *Recherches Philosophiques* entitled '*Hegel et Freud: essai d'une confrontation interprétative*'. A plan of the article, as well as fifteen pages written by Kojève, were found by his biographer, Dominique Auffret, amongst his papers after his death. Crucially, Kojève credits Hegel for having substituted the philosophy of the '*I think*' of Descartes with a philosophy of the '*I desire*'. See E. Roudinesco, op. cit., 147–9.

20. J. Lacan, S IV 303.

21. A. Kojève, *Introduction à la lecture de Hegel*, 12/5.

22. J. Lacan, S II 261/223–4.

23. J. Lacan, S VIII 102/79–80; S II 261/223–4.

24. M. Bowie, *Lacan*, op. cit., 137.

25. J. Lacan, E 627/524.

26. J. Lacan, S VIII, 242–4/200–2.

27. J. Lacan, E, 268/222. It's also because he identifies 'belief' (croyance) and 'desire' as the two basic mechanisms of society, and the 'laws' of imitation as the fundamental laws of society, that Gabriel Tarde rejects the idea of a natural, criminal instinct.

28. M. Bowie, *Lacan*, op. cit., 135.

29. M. Bowie, *Lacan*, op. cit., 136.

30. J. Lacan, E 691/580.

31. A. Kojève, op. cit., 13; Lacan, S I 169/172; E, 113, 121/92, 98–9. See also René Girard, *Mensonge romantique et vérité romanesque* (Paris: Grasset, 1961) and *La violence et le sacré* (Paris: Grasset, 1972).

32. J. Lacan, S XI 153/168.

33. M. Bowie, *Lacan*, op. cit, 52–3.

34. J. Lacan, S XI 182, 184–5/162, 164.

35. J. Lacan, E 803/680; S VII 132; S XX, 102/112–13.

36. J. Lacan, E 825/699.

37. J. Lacan, S XI 172, 197, 296/154, 176, 266.

38. For a genealogy of the connection between desire and recognition, see Miguel de Beistegui, *The Government of Desire: A Genealogy of the Liberal Subject* (Chicago: Chicago University Press, 2018), Chapter 6.

39. Deborah Luepnitz, 'Beyond the Phallus: Lacan and Feminism', *The Cambridge Companion to Lacan*, edited by J. M. Rabaté (Cambridge: Cambridge University Press, 2003), 226.

40. M. Bowie, *Lacan*, op. cit., 147.

41. Having said that, I should emphasize that, moving away from that phallocentrism of the 1950s, Lacan attempts to construct a distinctive and irreducible 'feminine sexuality' in his later work, and in the central chapter of *Encore*, the twentieth volume of his *Seminar*. See J. Lacan, 'God and Woman's *jouissance*', S XX 61–71/64–77; S XVIII 142–4. See also M. Bowie, *Lacan*, op. cit., 150–7.

42. J. Lacan, E 694/582–3; S III, 198/176. See also M. Borch-Jacobsen, *Lacan: The Absolute Master*, op. cit., 256–9.

43. J. Lacan, S II 315/272.

44. J. Lacan, S III 199/176. Translation modified.

45. Surprisingly, Adriana Cavarero doesn't discuss the case of Lacan in her critique of the *homo erectus* and the male paradigm of rectitude, to which she opposes a model of (female) inclination. See Adriana Cavarero, *Inclinations: a Critique of Rectitude*, translated by Amanda Minervini and Adam Sitze (Stanford: Stanford University Press, 2016). Kristeva is also insufficiently critical: like Lacan, she sees the symbolic, phallic order as an 'implacable structure' signalling the transition from natural to social being, and the primary defence against psychosis. Elizabeth Grosz is more critical of Lacan's position, and of its feminist defenders, in *Jacques Lacan: a Feminist Introduction* (New York and London: Routledge, 1990), 122–6. For a genuine feminist critique of the phallic position and, more generally, of Lacan on sexual difference, see Toril Moi, 'From Femininity to Finitude: Freud, Lacan, and Feminism, Again', *Signs: Journal of Women in Culture and Society*, 2004, vol. 29, no. 3, especially 853–4 (on the phallus) and 859–64 (on the meaning of feminine *jouissance* in Seminar XX). For a brief history and nuanced account of the reception of Lacan amongst feminist thinkers and clinicians in France and North America, see Deborah Luepnitz, 'Beyond the Phallus: Lacan and Feminism', op. cit., 221–37.

Chapter Two

1. J. Lacan, E 110/90.

2. Such as André Brouillet's *A Clinical Lesson at La Salpêtrière* (given by Charcot), from 1894, in which a hysterical woman (naturally!) is represented under hypnosis, and before an assembly of men, or Kokoschka's play *Mörder, Hoffnung der Frauen*, written in 1909, which features an equally hysterical woman protagonist.

3. J. Lacan, 'Structure des psychoses paranoïaques', *Semaine des hôpitaux de Paris*, 7.7.1931, 437–45. Lacan's article was published again in *Ornicar?*, 44,

Spring 1988, 5–18. Lacan acknowledges his debt to Clérambault in his doctoral thesis (PP 71–3), and then again in S III 13–14/5–6.

4. J. Lacan, E 65, 168/51, 137.

5. See Gaëtan Gatian de Clérambault, 'Les délires passionnels. Érotomanie, Revenidication, Jalousie' (Présentation de malade), and 'Érotomanie pure. Érotomanie associée' (Présentation de malade), *Bulletin de la Société Clinique de Médecine Mentale*, February 1921. Clérambault's psychiatric writings are available in *Œuvres psychiatriques* (Paris: Frénésie Éditions, 1998), volumes 1 and 2. See also Elisabeth Roudinesco, *Jacques Lacan. Esquisse d'une vie, histoire d'un système de pensée* (Paris: Fayard, 1993), 46.

6. See Salvador Dalí, 'The Rotting Donkey' ('L'âne pourri'), *Oui: The Paranoid-Critical Revolution. Writings 1927–1933*, edited by Robert Descharnes, translated by Yvonne Shafir (Boston: Exact Change: 1988), 115–19. On the significance of Dali's paranoid-critical method, and of Surrealism more generally, for the early Lacan, see J. M. Rabaté, Lacan's Turn to Freud, in J. M. Rabaté (ed.), *The Cambridge Companion to Lacan* (Cambridge: Cambridge University Press, 2003), 17–22.

7. Descartes' famous remarks on madness can be found in *Meditations on First Philosophy*, translated by Donald A. Cress, 14. A representative of the Cartesian school of psychiatry is Henri Ey, author of *Hallucinations et Délire* (Paris: Alcan, 1934), whom Lacan criticizes in 'Presentation on Psychical Causality' (1946), *Écrits*, 163–5/133–5. Rather than error, he claims, we need to attribute madness to misrecognition (*méconnaissance*).

8. See J. Lacan, S VII 42–3/32–3.

9. S. Freud, 'De quelques mécanismes névrotiques dans la jalousie, la paranoïa et l'homosexualité', translated by Jacques Lacan, *Revue françaize de psychanalyse*, 1932, V. The English version of the article can be found in S. Freud, SE XVIII, 223–32. Further articles on psychosis and paranoia include 'The Neuro-Psychoses of Defence' (1894) and 'Further Remarks on the Neuro-Psychoses of Defence' (1896) in SE III, 41–61 and 162–85. See also Freud's long analysis of Dr. jur. Daniel Paul Schreber's *Memoirs of a Nerve Patient* (1903), 'Psycho-Analytic Notes on an Autobiographical Account of a Case of Paranoia (*Dementia Paranoides*)' (1911), in SE XII, 9–82.

10. S. Freud, SE XVIII, 225.

11. J. Lacan, *De la psychose paranoïaque dans ses rapports avec la personnalité* [1932] (Paris: Éditions du Seuil, 1975).

12. For a detailed account of the case, see J. Lacan, *De la psychose paranoïaque*, op. cit., 247–350, and E. Roudinesco, op. cit., 55–79. J. M. Rabaté also emphasizes the significance of the case for the formation of Lacan's thought in 'Lacan's The Turn to Freud', Freud', in J. M. Rabaté (ed.), The *Cambridge Companion to Lacan* (Cambridge: Cambridge University Press, 2003), 12–17. Naturally, Aimée's action could be read entirely differently, and critically, from the point of view of sexual difference and patriarchy, and by emphasizing that homophobia is still pervasive in Lacan's diagnosis.

13. J. Lacan, 'Motifs du crime paranoïaque: le crime des sœurs Papin', *Le Minotaure*, 3/4, 1933: 25–8.

14. J. Lacan, E 151–93/123–60; E 100–24/82–101.

15. See J. Lacan, *Psychoses* (S III) and 'On a Question Prior to any treatment of Psychosis' (E 531–83/445–88).

16. See M. Klein, 'Notes on Some Schizoid Mechanisms' (1946) and 'on Identification' (1955), in *The Writings of Melanie Klein. Volume III. Envy and Gratitude and Other works 1946–1963*, under the general editorship of Roger Money-Kyrle (New York: The Free Press, 1975). On Lacan's opposition to the (largely American) theory of ego-psychology, and his early theory of the constitution of the subject of desire through projective identifications, and the mirror stage in particular, see Élisabeth Roudinesco, 'The Mirror Stage: An Obliterated Archive', translated by Barbara Bray, J. M. Rabaté (ed.), *The Cambridge Companion to Lacan* (Cambridge: Cambridge University Press, 2003), 28–30.

17. See J. Lacan, 'Le Symbolique, l'Imaginaire et le Réel', *Bulletin de l'Association freudienne*, 1, 1982, 4–13; 'Fonction et champ de la parole et du langage en psychanalyse' (E 237–322/197–268); 'Discours de Rome' (AE 133–64).

18. J. Lacan, E 114–15/92–3.

19. J. Lacan, S III 99/85–6.

20. M. Borch-Jacobsen, *Lacan: The Absolute Master*, trans. Douglas Brick (Stanford: Stanford University Press, 1991), 40–1.

21. J. Lacan, S III 286/252.

22. J. Lacan, S III 236/209.

Chapter Three

1. J. Lacan and M. Cénac, 'A Theoretical Introduction to the Functions of Psychoanalysis in Criminology', in E 125–48/102–22. See also Lacan's summary of the responses given in the discussion that followed Lacan and Cénac's paper at the thirteenth conference of the Psychanalystes de Langue Française on 29 May 1950: J. Lacan, 'Prémisses à tout développement possible de la criminologie', AE 121–5.

2. S. Freud, SE IX, 114.

3. S. Freud, SE IX, 103.

4. S. Freud, SE IX, 104.

5. Cesare Beccaria, *On Crimes and Punishments and Other Writings*, edited by Richard Bellamy [1764] (Cambridge: Cambridge University Press, 1995), 113.

6. 'Pleasure and pain', Beccaria writes, 'are the motive forces of all sentient beings' (*On Crimes and Punishments*, 21).

7. C. Beccaria, *On Crimes and Punishments*, op. cit., 7.

8. C. Beccaria, *On Crimes and Punishments*, op. cit., 64.

9. S. Freud, SE IX, 107.

10. Editor's Note, SE IX, 102.

11. Franz Alexander and Hugo Staub, *Der Verbrecher und seine Richter* (Vienna: Internationaler Psychoanalytischer Verlag, 1929). Melanie Klein, 'Criminal Tendencies in Normal Children' (1927), in *Love, Guilt and Reparation And Other Works 1921–1945* (London: Vintage, 1988). Klein's paper was originally published in *The British Journal of Medical Psychology*, Volume 14, Issue 2, June 1927: 177–92.

12. M. Klein, 'Criminal Tendencies in Normal Children', opo. cit., 181.

13. M. Klein, 'On Criminality', in *Love, Guilt and Reparation And Other Works 1921–1945*, op. cit., 258–61. The paper was originally published in *The British Journal of Medical Psychology*, Volume 14, Issue 4, December 1934: 312–15.

14. M. Klein, 'On Criminality', op. cit., 258.

15. J. Lacan, S VII 373/324–5.

16. In his first lecture course at the Collège de France, as well as in a lecture from 1972 entitled 'Oedipal Knowledge', Foucault traces the emergence of this science of crime back to classical Greece, and most notably through a masterful reading of Sophocles' *Oedipus King*. See M. Foucault, *Lectures on the Will to Know: Lectures at the Collège de France, 1970–1971*, translated by Graham Burchell (London & New York: Palgrave MacMillan, 2012).

17. The question of psychoanalysis's relation to truth, and the meaning and role of truth in psychoanalytic practice and metapsychology, runs through Lacan's entire work. In addition to the article already mentioned, see 'Beyond the "Reality Principle"' (1938) in E 79–80/63–4; S I 288–90/261–5; 'The Freudian Thing' (1955) in E 401–36/334–63; S XI 293–7/136–8, and 'Science and Truth' (1965) in E 855–77/726–45. See also M. Borch-Jacobsen, *Lacan: The Absolute Master*, trans. Douglas Brick (Stanford: Stanford University Press, 1991), Chapters 4 and 5.

18. J. Lacan, E 870/738–9.

19. M. Foucault, *Lectures on the Will to Know*, op. cit., 9 and 16 December 1970.

20. Aristotle, *Metaphysics* 980a 21–4. In *The Basic Works of Aristotle*, edited, and with an introduction, by R. Mc Keon (New York, Random House, 1941).

21. The term 'master of truth' is borrowed from Marcel Detienne's *The Masters of Truth in Archaic Greece*, translated by Janet Lloyd (New York: Zone Books, 1996). For Foucault's interpretation of the play, and the place of truth within it, see 'Oedipal Knowledge' in M. Foucault, *Lectures on the Will to Know*, op. cit., 229–61.

22. J. Lacan, S XX 85/92.

23. A. Badiou, *Le Séminaire. Vérité et sujet, 1987–1988* (Paris: Fayard, 2017), 90. For Badiou, truth is not 'a feature of language or propositions [*fait de langue ou d'énoncé*]', but 'a process that follows an event [*un processus post-événementiel*], the rule of which is to produce something indiscernible' (19). As a result, he does not consider psychoanalysis a science. It is even less a politics, or an art. But is it a 'supplementary generic procedure', that is, a procedure that produces truths, irreducible to those I have just mentioned? Badiou leaves the question wide open (141–6). I would argue that it is, for reasons that will become apparent. Badiou returns to this question in his 1994–1995 seminar (*Le Séminaire. Lacan. L'antiphilosophie 3, 1994–1995* (Paris: Fayard, 2013), 34 ff. There, he explicitly identifies the *matheme* as the expression of the tension inherent to analytic discourse, that is, of the fact that it is a discourse of truth *and* the science of something that can't be known (*l'insu*) (36). It is through this truth beyond or in excess of propositional truth that the matheme touches on the real. The matheme, he says, is situated at the point at which science is at a dead-end, but this point is that of the real ('*le mathème va être en un point d'impasse, mais ce point d'impasse, c'est le point du réel*' (44).

24. J. Lacan, S VII 90/73.

25. J. Lacan, S XVI 204.

26. On this point, my reading differs from Badiou's, who understands the university discourse not as the discourse of science as such, or of positivism, but of its excesses and dogmaticism. As a result, he is able to present Lacan as a champion of rationalism and heir of the enlightenment.

27. Lacan, S XVI 48, 42.

28. M. Foucault, *Psychiatric Power. Lectures at the Collège de France, 1973–74*, translated by Graham Burchell (Basingstoke/New York: Palgrave Macmillan, 2006), 239–47.

29. See M. Foucault, 'Entretien avec Michel Foucault' (1971), *Dits et écrits*, vol. II (Paris: Quarto Gallimard, 1994), 168–9.

30. This claim puts me not so much at odds with, as on a different trajectory from, Badiou, who reads Lacan as an anti-philosopher, by virtue of his fundamentally or arche-scientific (*archiscientifique*) stance, expressed in his commitment to the *matheme*, and most visible in his seminars from the 1970s. I, on the other hand, am trying to situate Lacan's contribution on the subject of truth in relation to tendencies and morphologies of truth within the history of science (and, more specifically, of the 'social' and 'human' sciences), as well as philosophy.

31. J. Lacan, S VII 107/88–9.

32. J. Lacan and M. Cénac, E 138/113.

33. J. Lacan and M. Cénac, E 138/113.

34. See M. Foucault, *The Birth of the Clinic: An Archaeology of Medical Perception*, translated by A. M. Sheridan Smith (London: Tavistock, 1973), 107–9.

35. J. Lacan, AE, 442.

36. J. Lacan, AE, 509.

37. Claude Lévi-Strauss, *Les Structures élémentaires de la parenté* (Paris: Presses Universitaires de France, 1949).

38. Claude Lévi-Strauss, *Les Structures élémentaires de la parenté*, op. cit., 29.

39. J. Lacan and M. Cénac, E 130/106.

40. J. Lacan, S VII 207–8/176–7.

41. J. Lacan and M. Cénac, E 137/111–12. The reference to Kant's practical philosophy, which Lacan will develop at length in Seminar VII and 'Kant with Sade' (1963), and to which I'll return, is illuminating: the moral law is the product of the faculty of *desire* and is clearly distinguished from interest

and utility, as well as any empirical law. It is the formal and thus structuring role of the law in the economy of desire that is at issue here.

42. J. Lacan and M. Cénac, E 134/109–10.

43. See Patrick Singy, 'Sexuality and Liberalism', in *The Care of Life: Transdisciplinary Perspectives in Bioethics and Biopolitics*, edited by Miguel de Beistegui, Giuseppe Bianco and Marjorie Gracieuse (London: Rowman & Littlefield, 2014), 232–3; Miguel de Beistegui, *The Government of Desire: A Genealogy of the Liberal Subject* (Chicago: The University of Chicago Press, 2018), Chapter 4.

44. Richard von Krafft-Ebing, *Psychopathia Sexualis, with Special Reference to Contrary Sexual Instinct: A Medico-legal Study*, translated by Charles Gilbert Chaddock [1886] (Philadelphia: The F. A. Davis Company, 1893). The first treatise of psychiatry in German dedicated to sexuality and sexual abnormalities is Heinrich Kaan's own *Psychopathia Sexualis* (Leipzig, 1844).

45. J. Lacan and M. Cénac, E 147/120.

46. J. Lacan, S VII 219–20/187.

47. J. Lacan, S VII 220/187.

48. J. Lacan and M. Cénac, E 137–8/112. My emphasis.

49. J. Lacan and M. Cénac, E 149/122.

50. J. Lacan and M. Cénac, E 131/107.

51. J. Lacan, and M. Cénac, E 135/110.

52. It is important to bear in mind that, following the publication of Heidegger's *Letter on Humanism* in 1946, the dispute regarding the place and value of humanism in philosophy and the social sciences was in full swing at the time, and eventually triggered a backlash against both Sartrean and Marxist humanism, which also affected Lacan's thought.

53. M. Borch-Jacobsen, *Lacan: The Absolute Master*, op. cit., 158.

Chapter Four

1. See J. Lacan, S XI 247/221–2; E, 780/658–9.

2. See I. Kant, *Critique of Practical Reason*, translated and edited by Mary J. Gregor, in *The Cambridge Edition of the Works of Immanuel Kant. Practical*

Philosophy, (Cambridge: Cambridge University Press, 2002), 5: 20–2. The translation is based on the standard edition of Kant's works, *Kants gesammelte Schriften*, Königlich Preußische Akademie der Wissenschaften (Berlin: G. Reimer; Berlin and New York: Walter de Gruyter & Co. and Predecessors, 1902–), vol. 5, edited, with introduction, variant readings and factual elucidations, by Paul Natorp (1908).

3. J. Lacan, S VII 9/1.

4. J. Lacan, S VII 12/3.

5. Slavoj Žižek, *For They Know Not What They Do: Enjoyment as a Political Factor* (London: Verso, 1991), 239.

6. Georges Bataille, *Œuvres complètes* (Paris: Gallimard, 1971–1988), vol. III, 512. Cited by Slavoj Žižek in *The Parallax View* (Cambridge, MA: The MIT Press, 2006), 95.

7. For Bataille's readings of Sade, which extend over his entire work and several decades (1929–1957), and with which Lacan was quite familiar, see *Œuvres complètes*, op. cit., vol. II, 54–76, vol. VIII, 148–57, vol. IX 239–58, vol. X 176–95.

8. Augustine, *Confessions*, translated by W. Watts Book (Cambridge, MA: Harvard University Press, 1912), Book II, Chapter 9.

9. Augustine, *Confessions*, op. cit., Book II, Chapter 4.

10. Slavoj Žižek, *The Parallax View*, op. cit., 90–6.

11. See J. Lacan, S VII 208, 220, 229–30/176–7, 187, 195.

12. See J. Lacan, E 770/649–50.

13. I. Kant, *Critique of Practical Reason*, op. cit., 5: 110–12; 5: 116–19.

14. J. Lacan, S XX 10/2–3.

15. G. Bataille, *La part maudite I: la consumation*, in *Œuvres complètes*, op. cit., vol. VII, 248.

16. J. Lacan, S XX 10/2–3. In the following and concluding chapter, I will show how, in the late 1960s and early 1970s, Lacan understands *jouissance* quite differently, in the quasi-legal sense of use and enjoyment, captured in the idea of usufruct. By then, the defining feature of desire is no longer the law, but the complex status of the object, especially in the age of advanced capitalism.

17. J. Lacan, S XI 306/275. See also E. Roudinesco, 'Lacan et Spinoza, essai d'interprétation', in Olivier Bloch (ed.), *Spinoza au XXème siècle* (Paris: Presses Universitaires de France, 1992).

18. Dany Nobus, *The Law of Desire: On Lacan's 'Kant with Sade'* (Basingstoke: Palgrave Macmillan/Springer Nature, 2017), 39.

19. D. Nobus, *The Law of Desire*, op. cit., 39.

20. This idea, the perspicacity of which Lacan salutes in the final section of 'Kant with Sade', was introduced by Pierre Klossowski in *Sade mon prochain* (Paris: Éditions du Seuil, 1947).

21. J. Lacan, E 667/558–9. Translation modified.

22. Lorenzo Chiesa, cited by Žižek, *The Parallax View*, op. cit., 92.

23. J. Lacan, E, 69, 78/54, 62–3.

24. S. Žižek, *The Parallax View*, op. cit., 95.

25. D. Nobus, *The Law of Desire*, op. cit., 40–1.

26. J. Lacan, E 775/654, E 907/862.

27. S. Žižek, *The Parallax View*, op. cit., 92.

28. J. Lacan, S XVI 228.

29. Vladimir Safatle, *Grand Hotel Abyss: Desire, Recognition and the Restoration of the Subject* (Leuven: Leuven University Press, 2016), 91–2.

30. J. Lacan, S VII, 133/112. On courtly love, especially as an attempt to move beyond 'narcissistic love', see also J. Lacan, S XVI, 230–2.

31. Gen Doy, *Drapery: Classicism and Barbarism in Visual Culture* (London: I.B. Tauris, 2002), 106.

32. Cited in Gen Doy, *Drapery*, op. cit., 106.

33. The situation was, in fact, not as clear as Foucault seems to suggest. It's true that, on the whole, French psychoanalysts stayed clear of collaborating with the enemy in occupied France during World War II and avoided lending a hand to its biological racism. Marie Bonaparte, for example, through her exile and immediate support to the Jews, disabled any attempt to 'aryanize' the French psychoanalytical community. However, the situation was different in Germany, where, under the influence of Ernest Jones, a number of psychoanalysts decided to collaborate with the Nazis in order to 'save' psychoanalysis. On this question, see E. Roudinesco, 'Lacan et Spinoza, essai d'interprétation', op. cit., 119–21, 207–14.

34. See J. Lacan, 'La psychiatrie anglaise et la guerre', AE 101–20. The extraordinary level of engagement of German psychiatrists in setting up and carrying out the Nazi plans of eugenics, euthanasia and 'racial hygiene'

is now well documented. See Burkhart Brückner, *Basiswissen: Geschichte der Psychiatrie* (Bonn: Psychiatrie Verlag, 2010); Sheila Faith Weiss, *The Nazi Symbiosis: Human Genetics and Politics in the Third Reich* (Chicago: The University of Chicago Press, 2011); Prof. Dr. Dr. Frank Schneider (ed.), *Psychiatrie im Nationalsozialismus/Psychiatry under National Socialism* (Berlin/Heidelberg/New York: Springer, 2011).

35. M. Foucault, *The History of Sexuality, Volume 1: An Introduction*, translated by Robert Hurley (New York: Random House, 1978), 150.

36. See for example M. Foucault's 1976 interview, 'L'extension sociale de la norme' in *Dits et écrits*, vol. II (Paris: Quarto Gallimard, 2002), 75–6.

37. On the immunological paradigm, and its relation to Nazism, see Roberto Esposito, *Bíos: Biopolitics and Philosophy*, translated by Timothy Campbell (Minneapolis: University of Minnesota Press, 2008), and *Immunitas: The Protection and Negation of Life*, translated by Zakiya Hanafi (Cambridge: Polity Press, 2011).

38. M. Foucault, *The History of Sexuality, Volume 1*, op. cit., 83.

39. M. Foucault, *The History of Sexuality, Volume 1*, op. cit., 83.

40. M. Foucault, *The History of Sexuality, Volume 1*, op. cit., 90.

41. Gilles Deleuze and Félix Guattari, *Anti-Oedipus*, translated by Robert Hurley, Mark Seem and Helen R. Lane (London: Athlone, 1984), 112.

Chapter Five

1. J. Lacan, S XVI 36. The most detailed account of Lacan's position with the structuralist movement, and structuralist linguistics in particular, can be found in François Dosse, *History of Structuralism*, 2 vols. (Minneapolis: University of Minnesota Press, 1997). See also Dany Nobus, 'Lacan's Science of the Subject: Between Linguistics and Topology', *The Cambridge Companion to Lacan* (Cambridge: Cambridge University Press, 2003), 50–68. For less recent but still valuable accounts, see Richard Harland, *Superstructuralism: The Philosophy of Structuralism and Post-structuralism* (London: Methuen, 1987); Malcolm Bowie, 'Jacques Lacan', *Structuralism and Since: From Lévi-Strauss to Derrida*, edited by John Sturrock (Oxford: Oxford University Press, 1979); Fredric Jameson, *The Prison-House of Language: A Critical Account of Structuralism and Russian Formalism* (Princeton: Princeton University Press, 1979).

2. The proceedings of the conference, edited by Maurice de Gandillac, Lucien Goldmann and Jean Piaget, were published in 1965 (Éditions Mouton & Co). For a more recent edition, see M. de Gandillac, L. Goldmann and J. Piaget (eds.), *Entretiens sur les notions de genèse et de structure* (Paris: Hermann, 2011).

3. Lacan reiterates the uselessness of *jouissance*, and the difference that separates it from utility, in S XX 10/3.

4. '*Jouissance* makes the entire substance of what we speak about in psychoanalysis' (S XVI 45). Translation mine. 'The topology of *jouissance* is the topology of the subject' (S XVII 114/100).

5. For a systematic treatment of *jouissance* in Lacan, especially as distinct from desire *and* pleasure, see Néstor Braunstein, 'Desire and jouissance in the teachings of Lacan', translated from the Spanish by Tamara Francés, *The Cambridge Companion to Lacan*, op. cit., 102–15. Braunstein's account, however, does not deal with Seminars XVI and XVII, which introduce the idea of the *plus-de-jouir*, on which I will focus.

6. Playing on the French *à cause*, or because, Lacan also refers to the object *a* as *a-cause* (S XVI 119).

7. J. Lacan, S XX 114/126–7.

8. J. Lacan, S XVII 56/50.

9. J. Lacan, S XI 164/146. See also R. Bernet, *Force – Pulsion – Désir. Une autre philosophie de la psychanalyse* (Paris: Vrin, 2013), 238–9.

10. J. Lacan, S XVII 54/48.

11. J. Lacan, S XVII 52/46.

12. On Lacan's reading of the role of *agalma* in Platos' *Symposium*, see S VIII 167–99. In his 1948 article, 'La notion mythique de la valeur en Grèce', Louis Gernet shows how the term *agalma* 'refers to various types of objects, including human beings, as "precious"' (L. Gernet, *Anthropologie de la Grèce antique* [Paris: François Maspero, 1968], 127). It expresses an idea of wealth, and especially noble wealth (horses are *algamata*), and is inseparable from the idea, contained in the verb *agallein*, which means at once to ornament and to honour. Furthermore, as property of the gods, *agalma* are thought to be sacred goods and their theft sacrilegious (128–9). Still according to Gernet, the 'inherent virtue' of *agalma* is its '"social" power', in other words its fetish-like power (176).

13. J. Lacan, S XVII 56/50. Translation modified.

14. J. Lacan, S XVII 19/19. Translation modified.

15. J. Lacan, S XVII 18/18.

16. J. Lacan, S XX 13/7.

17. J. Lacan, S XX 10/3. Translation modified.

18. On the 'replacement' of structural linguistics by non-spherical topology as the structure itself, freed of all metaphor, see Lacan's 1972 text 'L'Étourdit', *Scilicet 4* (1973), especially 28, 40. On the limits of this replacement, or displacement, see D. Nobus, 'Lacan's Science of the Subject', op. cit., 63–5.

19. J. Lacan, S XVI 48.

20. J-P. Cléro, *Dictionnaire Lacan* (Paris: ellipses, 2008), 64.

21. S. Freud, 'Constructions in Analysis', translated by James Strachey, SE 23: 261.

22. S. Freud, SE 23, 259.

23. S. Freud, SE 23, 267.

24. S. Freud, SE 23, 268.

25. J. Lacan, S I 26–7/13.

26. J. Lacan, S XVI 45.

27. J. Lacan, 'Radiophonie. Réponses à sept questions posées par M. Robert Georgin pour la radiodiffusion belge', 1970, in AE 434.

28. J. Lacan, S XVI 18.

29. Ibid.

30. For an in-depth discussion of this question, and one I'll be referring to on several occasions, see S. Tomšič, *The Capitalist Unconscious: Marx and Lacan* (London: Verso, 2015).

31. J. Lacan, S XVI 21.

32. S. Tomšič, *The Capitalist Unconscious*, op. cit., 103.

33. S. Tomšič, *The Capitalist Unconscious*, op. cit., 92.

34. S. Tomšič, *The Capitalist Unconscious*, op. cit., 103–4.

35. Slavoj Žižek, *Incontinence of the Void: Economico-Philosophical Spandrels* (Cambridge, MA: The MIT Press, 2017), 230.

36. S. Tomšič, *The Capitalist Unconscious*, op. cit., 89–91. Psychoanalysis, Tomšič argues, suffered a similar fate 'when the Post-Freudians recentralised the

subject on the ego and deduced from Freud's *Wo es war soll Ich werden* an imperative of normalisation' largely implemented through the International Psychoanalytic Association, 'the psychoanalytic equivalent of the Stalinist Party' (91). It is the same subject, namely, the subject of ego psychology, institutionalized and normalized, which Deleuze and Guattari target in *Anti-Oedipus*, and to which they oppose the 'true' subject of desire in the form of the schizophrenic. See also E. Roudinesco, *Lacan, envers et contre tout* (Paris: Seuil, 2011), 32–3.

37. Jacques Rancière, *Dissensus: On Politics and Aesthetics*, translated by Steven Corcoran (London: Bloomsbury, 2010), 53.

38. S. Tomšič, *The Capitalist Unconscious*, op. cit., 61.

39. K. Marx, *Grundrisse. Foundations of the Critique of Political Economy* (Rough Draft), translated by M. Nicolaus (London: Penguin Books in association with *New Left Review*, 1973), 222.

40. Slavoj Žižek, *Incontinence of the Void*, op. cit., 180.

41. J. Lacan, S XVI 39.

42. J. Lacan, S XI 301/270.

43. S. Tomšič, *The Capitalist Unconscious*, op. cit. 215.

44. J. Lacan, S XVI, 249.

45. J. Lacan, S XVII 124/108.

46. J. Lacan, 'Radiophonie', AE 434.

47. J. Lacan, 'Radiophonie', AE 435.

48. J. Lacan, 'Radiophonie', AE 435.

49. Slavoj Žižek, *Incontinence of the Void*, op. cit., 167.

50. J. Lacan, S XVI 48.

51. Lacan, S XVI 42.

52. Bruce Fink, *The Lacanian Subject: Between Language and Jouissance* (Princeton: Princeton University Press, 1995), 133.

53. J. Lacan, S XVI 40.

54. J. Lacan, S XVI 41.

55. J. Lacan, S VII 12/3.

56. J. Lacan, S XVI 30.

57. J. Lacan, S XVI 239/242.

58. G. Deleuze, 'Desire and Pleasure', *Two Regimes of Madness. Texts and Interviews 1975–1995*, translated by Ames Hodges and Mike Taormina (Los Angeles: Semiotext(e), 2006), 124.

Chapter Six

1. Georges Canguilhem, *The Normal and the Pathological*, translated by Carolyn R. Fawcett and Robert S. Cohen (New York: Zone Books, 1998), 33. Translation modified.

2. J. Lacan, S XXIII, 42/31.

3. J. Lacan, S XXII, 164–5.

4. J. Lacan, S XXII 178; E, 817/692.

5. J. Lacan, S XXII, 97, 101, 112 and 114.

6. G. Deleuze, 'La littérature et la vie', in *Critique et clinique* (Paris: Les Éditions de Minuit, 1993), 11.

7. M. Blanchot, *L'écriture du désastre* (Paris: Gallimard, 1980), 71–2.

8. M. Blanchot, *Le pas au-delà* (Paris: Gallimard, 1973), 91.

9. 'The poem', Char writes, is 'the realised love of the desire that's remained desire [*l'amour réalisé du désir demeuré désir*]'. Cited by M. Blanchot, *L'espace littéraire* (Paris: Gallimard, 1955), 250.

10. 'Conversation with Michel Foucault' (a conversation with Duccio Trombadori), in Dits et écrits, vol. II (Paris: Quarto Gallimard, 2001), no. 128: 862.

11. Ibid.

INDEX

Lightning Source UK Ltd.
Milton Keynes UK
UKHW022040110122
396947UK00003B/297